Twayne's United States Authors Series

Sylvia E. Bowman, *Editor*

INDIANA UNIVERSITY

Vardis Fisher

VARDIS FISHER

by Joseph M. Flora
University of North Carolina

Twayne Publishers, Inc.   ::   New York

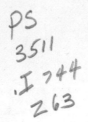

MANUFACTURED IN THE UNITED STATES OF AMERICA BY
UNITED PRINTING SERVICES, INC.
NEW HAVEN, CONN.

To
JOE LEE DAVIS
RADCLIFFE SQUIRES
ARTHUR J. CARR
ARTHUR M. EASTMAN

Preface

THOMAS WOLFE'S literary agent and later his biographer and editor of his letters, Elizabeth Nowell, took a tip from Wolfe in 1935 and wrote to a fairly obscure writer from Idaho to inquire if she could serve as his agent.[1] Miss Nowell was interested in literature and in the serious writer, and Wolfe had said that Vardis Fisher was her man. Thus, the hard-working lady from New England became the agent and friend of another unusual and energetic novelist, one whom critics and readers were to compare constantly with Wolfe.[2]

These two dynamos, both instructors at New York University, were friends and protective of each other because they felt a spiritual kinship. While Miss Nowell was preparing *The Letters of Thomas Wolfe,* she wrote Fisher that he was one of the few writers Wolfe had never criticized: "I think he felt that you had never got the recognition you deserved, and that was one reason he was always FOR you, suggesting you to me (tho that was as much for my sake as yours or more), 'talking you up' to Rowohlt... Think he identified you with himself, sort of: two guys trying to write books from really inside, and long series of them, and so up against it to get recognized for what they were."[3]

Actually, Fisher had made a rather propitious beginning as a novelist. His first two novels, though not best sellers, were highly praised; and critics expected a rich new regionalist contribution to American literature. When Fisher started his autobiographical tetralogy, he still seemed in the regionalist tradition, but it was soon evident that the modern Rousseau had other things in mind. The tetralogy shot Fisher into fame with the *litterati,* even if they did not always approve him. When *Children of God* won the Harper prize in 1939, Fisher was, from all indications, in the forefront of American letters.

Before he had finished his tetralogy and while he was writing *Children of God,* Fisher conceived the scheme for a long series of novels which would show the development of man's mind and spirit. While reviewers and the public were praising the Mormon saga, Fisher was trying to talk up his scheme with publishers, with very little success. When the first few books of the new series appeared, a few critics noticed them with interest. However, they received nothing like the attention Fisher got in the depression decade. Even his first two novels received more notice. But midway through the series, Fisher was receiving almost no attention. He had become a historical curiosity; he was dismissed as a writer whose interest belonged essentially to the troubled decade of the 1930's. Indeed, it seemed for a time that *The Testament of Man* would not even be published. But Fisher kept writing, hopeful that someday the books would find a public.

If one compares Fisher's reputation with Wolfe's, as Miss Nowell suggests, one finds that Fisher had much the worse time of it. Wolfe's acclaim and fame were greater than Fisher's from the start. And, although Wolfe's reputation diminished, it never declined as much as Fisher's, and it has in recent years experienced a modest revival.

It now seems possible to view Vardis Fisher—who like Wolfe has been accused of being too autobiographical and of surrendering to a gigantic energy and producing sprawling work—with a new detachment. The debates which surrounded Fisher have subsided, and his reputation is also undergoing a modest revival. Most of his books, including the entire *Testament*, are available in paperback, and a new scattering of critical attention in periodicals is in evidence. The September, 1963, issue of *The American Book Collector*, for instance, is a special Vardis Fisher number.

The highest ambition of this study is to assist in the inevitable re-evaluation of Fisher's works. It is not exhaustive, but it gives a survey of the world of his fiction; points out major themes; and explores the artistic accomplishments as they serve or hinder these themes. This study is only incidentally biographical, but Chapter 1 (as complete a biography of Fisher as is presently published) outlines the chief struggles of Fisher's life in anticipation of a study of his autobiographical fiction, which is, as in Wolfe's case, pivotal. Fisher's philosophical and artistic positions are thus made clear for consideration of the rest of his work: *The Testament of Man* (Chapter 4), his novels of the Antelope country of Idaho (Chapter 5), and his American historical novels (Chapter 6). The concluding chapter assesses the total range of his work and his place in American letters.

The University of North Carolina   JOSEPH M. FLORA
Chapel Hill, September, 1963

Acknowledgments

I am greatly indebted to the Graduate School of the University of North Carolina for a research grant in connection with the writing of this book. I am also indebted to Professors Joe Lee Davis, Radcliffe Squires, and Robert Haugh for their advice and interest in the project and to Professor Sylvia E. Bowman for her interest and thoughtful editing. I should like also to acknowledge my indebtedness to Yale University Library for allowing me to use the Fisher papers in the Yale Collection of American Literature. Miss Ruth Brend and Mrs. Nancy Smith graciously helped with typing chores. To my wife, Christine, I owe a special debt for her patience and critical eye. Vardis and Opal Fisher were obliging hosts for a personal interview. In addition Mr. Fisher has kindly answered my correspondence and granted me full permission to quote from his work.

I wish also to make further acknowledgment to the following:

To Alan Swallow for his permission to quote from the *Testament of Man.*

To Doubleday and Company, Inc., for permission to quote from *Tale of Valor*, copyright 1958; *Pemmican*, copyright 1956; *Love and Death*, copyright 1959.

To Vanguard Press, Inc., for permission to quote from *Children of God*, copyright 1939.

To Harcourt, Brace & World, Inc., for permission to quote from *Aspects of the Novel* by E. M. Forster, copyright 1927, 1954.

To The Viking Press for permission to quote from *The Liberal Imagination* by Lionel Trilling, copyright 1950.

To Charles Scribner's Sons for permission to quote from Wolfe's letter of June 7, 1938, in *The Letters of Thomas Wolfe,* ed. by Elizabeth Nowell, copyright 1956.

To Mrs. Alice H. Brewer, guardian of the minor children of Elizabeth Nowell, for permission to quote from the unpublished letters of Elizabeth Nowell.

To W. B. Thorsen for permission to use my article "The Early Power of Vardis Fisher," which appeared in *The American Book Collector*, September, 1963, issue, as a part of Chapter 5 in this volume.

Contents

Chronology

1895 Vardis Fisher born in Annis, Idaho, March 31.

1901 Moved to isolated river basin home.

1915 Graduated from Rigby High School, Rigby, Idaho.

1917 Married Leona McMurtrey, September 10.

1918 Birth of son, Grant; drafted into U. S. Army; corporal.

1920 Bachelor of Arts, University of Utah.

1921 Birth of son, Wayne.

1922 Master of Arts, University of Chicago.

1924 Death of Leona McMurtrey Fisher, September 8.

1925 Ph. D. *(magna cum laude)* University of Chicago.

1925- Assistant professor in English, University of Utah.
1928

1927 *Sonnets to an Imaginary Madonna.*

1928 Married Margaret Trusler; *Toilers of the Hills.*

1928- Assistant professor in English, Washington Square Col-
1931 lege, New York University.

1930 Summer in Europe.

1931 Returned to Idaho ranch; *Dark Bridwell.*

1932 *In Tragic Life;* taught summer at Montana State University.

1933 Taught summer at Montana State University.

1934 *Passions Spin the Plot.*

1935 *We Are Betrayed.*

1935- Director, Idaho Writers' Project and Historical Records
1939 Project of Works Progress Administration.

1936 *No Villain Need Be.*

1937 *April;* birth of son, Thornton Roberts.

1938 *Forgive Us Our Virtues.*

1939 *Children of God;* wins Harper Prize for Fiction; Divorced from Margaret.

1940 Married Opal Laurel Holmes.

1941 *City of Illusion.*

1943 *The Mothers; Darkness and the Deep,* first volume of *Testament of Man.*

1944 *The Golden Rooms.*

1946 *Intimations of Eve.*

1947 *Adam and the Serpent.*

1948 *The Divine Passion.*

1951 *The Valley of Vision.*

1952 *The Island of the Innocent.*

1953 *God or Caesar?;* trip to Europe, autumn and early winter, 1953-54.

1956 Alan Swallow assumes publication of *Testament; Jesus Came Again; A Goat for Azazel; Pemmican.* Trip to Europe and Middle East, autumn and early winter, 1956-57.

1957 *Peace Like a River.*

1958 *My Holy Satan; Tale of Valor;* trip to Europe, autumn and early winter, 1958-59.

1959 *Love and Death,* collected short stories.

1960 *Orphans in Gethsemane,* last volume of *Testament,* published.

1962 *Suicide or Murder?*

1963 *Thomas Wolfe As I Knew Him and Other Essays.*

Vardis Fisher

CHAPTER 1

The Frontier Shapes a Novelist

A S TWENTIETH-CENTURY AMERICA has hastened toward an increasingly urbanized society, Vardis Fisher's
life appears increasingly anachronistic.[1] His early background
hardly seems of our time. Born and reared on one of the last
primitive frontiers—Annis, Idaho, a sparsely settled community
of Mormons who were pioneering in the upper Snake River
Valley as a part of the church's practical program of expansion—
he was partly blessed and partly cursed with a heritage that
enabled him as a writer to understand the course of a turbulent
young America, as the genteel tradition had not allowed it to
be recorded.

The first child of the union of Temperance Thornton Fisher
and Joseph Oliver Fisher, young Vardis saw little affection
between his parents.[2] His father was a gruff strong-bodied,
strong-willed man who hated civilization. Vardis says that his
father was typical of the frontiersmen he has known, but his
mother was a proud woman of English ancestry who despised
the backwoods and who longed to make her mark in the world—
a goal she set for herself in her two sons. The desire to see
her sons famous and influential sustained her scarcely ideal
marriage, for she persuaded her husband to share her dream
and the violent labor necessary to achieve it. Work was the
highest virtue in the Fisher household—almost a religion in
itself. Fisher, who gets his own drive honestly, has praised
the determination of his parents as representative of the spirit
that made this nation.

When Vardis was six, he and his family—including a brother,
Vivian Ezra, and a baby sister, Viola Irene—moved into the
Big Hole mountain region on the South Fork of Snake River.
Their new mountain-surrounded home was thirty miles from

the civilization his father hated; their only neighbor within eight or ten miles was the Wheaton family across the river. Fisher says his father might as well have moved to the other side of the world. He suspects that his mother agreed to the move only to escape her hectoring mother-in-law, who relished all of the vulgarity repulsive to Temperance's strict codes.

In the Antelope Hills the Fishers encountered a world of sagebrush, wind, coyote, bear, wolf, cougar—and loneliness. They lived on the river bottom land, and then grubbed a living from the wild country about them. They had no luxuries. Their bed coverings were deer and elk skins, and their diet was dependent on the wild animals and wild fruits about them. Rather than an idyllic paradise, their new home meant to Vardis loneliness, fear, death, and labor as a first law.

For five years Vardis did not leave the sunken basin. He grew up silent and afraid. He and his brother were schooled by the ambitious Temperance and molded by her unbending moral strictures. Later the boys boarded a year with relatives in order to attend a crude frontier school. The fearful and unimposing Vardis had to develop physical prowess to defend his brother. Vivian attracted the ridicule of the school's bullies not only because he too was morbidly shy and frightened, but especially because he was cross-eyed.

In order to attend high school, Vardis at sixteen lived outside Rigby, Idaho, with Vivian in a small concrete hut; here he began to lose his fear and to enter the world of people. Mainly unsuccessful in his efforts to merge himself into a larger humanity, he wrote poetry and a melodramatic novel like those he had read frequently in the lonely basin home. The world of books became larger for him, but his mind was tortured with all of the why's of existence. He left the Mormon Church at eighteen, refusing to go on a missionary call and precipitating a major emotional crisis involving a sexual conflict, a conflict he weathered with the help of an understanding high school teacher, Thomas B. Matney. Because of his heritage and extremely lonely first years, Fisher developed a sense of humor much later than do most people. Consequently, he had few reserves for meeting the realities of the world, the flesh, and the devil. Adolescence was even more painful for Fisher than it is for most people.

When he entered the University of Utah after high school graduation, he still had little defense against the world. In Salt Lake City, center of the Mormon Church he had left, Vardis was as lonely and frustrated as ever. He had no faith to replace the lost one; he was not adept at making friends, and he was increasingly burdened by his sexuality. Thus he found his warmest refuge in books. Of course, he felt a strong obligation to do well in school in order to repay the sacrifices he knew his parents were making for his education. He worked in part-time jobs and pinched pennies in painful Horatio Alger style. After his second year at Utah and without having solved the problems which were perplexing him, he married his child-hood sweetheart, Leona McMurtrey, who was ill-equipped to meet the stern demands of her young husband's search for satisfying intellectual and moral codes.

Fisher's education was disrupted for service in World War I, first as an enlisted officer candidate in the Air Force, from which he resigned, and later as a draft volunteer in the army. He became a corporal, but the war ended and his regiment was dismissed without having been overseas.

With his wife and son, Fisher returned to Salt Lake City to finish his Bachelor of Arts degree. At Utah he received high praise for the plays he was writing and became convinced that his future was in teaching and writing; consequently, he started graduate work at the University of Chicago. Fisher found the Chicago experience demanding and—complicated by marital problems—a dreadful period in his life. But he came to view the training as a major force in the preparation for the writer that was to be. Four noted scholars at Chicago were particularly influential in teaching him the demands of scholarship, and in appreciation he dedicated his novel *Valley of Vision* to them: John Matthews Manly, Robert Morss Lovett, James Root Hulbert, and George Sherburn. These men taught Fisher, as he is fond of saying, "to respect the integrity of a fact and the privileged position of a probability." He did his Master's thesis on Daniel Defoe and London low life, his main interest having shifted from the drama to the novel. He received the degree in 1922. In 1925 he received his doctorate (*magna cum laude*); his dissertation was on the literary reputation of a writer he greatly admires, George Meredith. For one year of this time Fisher was a teaching fellow and taught freshmen composition. He also read himself almost blind. John Matthews Manly called him a "book drunkard."

But before the day when Manly put his arm around Fisher after his doctoral orals to tell him that he should be a better novelist for having learned what scholarship is, Fisher's life was almost completely ruined by the grief caused by his wife Leona's suicide on September 8, 1924, a date which Fisher still considers the most decisive and most painful of his life. For as he makes abundantly clear, it was his own failure to make sense of his life that had led Leona to this step. With the help of his psychologist brother, Fisher overcame his own desire for death and with painful honesty examined his past in an effort to purge his life of its pretenses. As a result of this experience, almost all of his writings—from the *Sonnets to an Imaginary Madonna,* which reflects the ruinous marriage, to the end of the *Testament of Man*—deal with the theme of uncovering man's evasions.

But if Fisher had learned to see himself more clearly, he had not learned to make that self more acceptable in society. His program of self-inspection and intellectual honesty got him into increasingly serious trouble at the University of Utah, where he was an assistant professor in English from 1925-28; for he was never silent about his intellectual quests. He acquired a rather infamous campus reputation. He was frequently misquoted, and many people were willing to believe anything about their unorthodox teacher. At the same time, Fisher felt hampered by the pressures of the Mormon community upon administrators and, thence, himself. In his demand for a pure gospel of truth, he was as rigid a Puritan as his mother could ever have been. To find the intellectual freedom he needed, Fisher resigned from the University of Utah and accepted a position as assistant professor at New York University.

At Washington Square College of New York University, Fisher, who had just published his first novel, was but one of several promising young teachers. The group included Hal White, Eda Lou Walton, Frederic Prokosch, Margaret Schlauch, Edwin Burgham, Leonie Adams, William Troy, and, most significantly, Thomas Wolfe. Fisher wrote: "I had more in common with him than I have ever had with another friend."[3]

Fisher was not influenced by Wolfe in the same way that he was by other writers who formed his literary taste: Keats, Meredith, France, Cabell. But Wolfe's huge autobiographical novel may have led Fisher to write his autobiographical novels sooner than he had planned. Perhaps Wolfe became most significant for Fisher as a symbol of the artist-child, a point to be illustrated in succeeding chapters. Russell Krauss reports an amusing sidelight on Wolfe's and Fisher's evaluations of each other's works: each felt the other had written himself out autobiographically.[4]

Shortly before his death, Wolfe tried unsuccessfully to locate Fisher on his journey to the West. While in Idaho he sensed what the country could do to one and what it had done to Fisher. On June 7, 1938, he wrote from Boise to Elizabeth Nowell:

> What I saw . . . is the abomination of desolation: an enormous desert bounded by infinitely-far-away mountains that you never get to, and little pitiful blistered towns huddled down in the most abject loneliness underneath the huge light and scale and weather and the astounding brightness and dimensions of everything—all given a kind of tremendousness and terror and majesty. And this?—their pride and joy, I guess, set in a cup of utterly naked hills, a clean little town but with a sparseness, a lack of the color, open-ness, richness of Cheyenne. I've tried to find Fisher: people know him here but he's not in the telephone book. Anyway, what I've seen today explains a lot about him.[5]

This wild Idaho country was strong in Fisher's blood, and he returned to it and to his two sons in 1931. Even though he had found a new freedom at New York University, his real drive, like Wolfe's, was for writing, not for teaching; but during two depression summers he taught at Montana State University primarily for financial reasons.[6] After his return to his homeland, he built his parents a modern house and farm buildings—and he wrote. With him was Margaret Trusler Fisher, who had been a fellow student at the University of Chicago and whom he had married in 1928. Fisher was hard at work on the autobiographical tetralogy which made his name known—though not always admired—in literary circles.

Two novels preceded the tetralogy: *Toilers of the Hills* and *Dark Bridwell.* Both had received enthusiastic reviews, though neither made their author famous or wealthy. Furthermore, Fisher could not find a publisher for *In Tragic Life* (1932) because, as one stated, "it was too strong meat" for their table.[7] Fisher found himself in the midst of a fight for a franker treatment of sex in literature. It was not until 1933 that Joyce's *Ulysses* could come to America. The brave firm which came to Fisher's rescue was the Caxton Press of Idaho. After *In Tragic Life* made such a stir, Eastern publishers wrote Fisher asking why he had not sent them the novel! Caxton was to come to Fisher's aid repeatedly until it, too, abandoned him in the midst of the *Testament of Man*. Problems with publishers have plagued him for almost his whole career.

To relieve the financial pinch, Fisher in 1935 accepted the position of director of the Federal Writers' Project of the Works Progress Administration in Idaho. *The Idaho Guide, Idaho Encyclopedia,* and *Idaho Folklore* are almost entirely his work. Fisher made Idaho the pace-setter for the nation in a project which Lewis Mumford called "the finest contribution to American patriotism that has been made in our generation."[8] E. Current-Garcia says Idaho published "despite its limited staff, about twice as much creditable material as any other state Project, except perhaps New York's."[9] Fisher finally resigned because of his disgust over the incompetence and waste by project officials.

When not racing around the state or region (for Fisher was later given duties in other Western states) researching for the project, he was researching for and writing novels. Like his parents, he was never bound by the concept of the eight-hour day. He received the first generous recompense for his Herculean labors with the widely hailed saga of the Mormons, *Children of God,* which won the Harper prize for fiction ($10,000) in 1939. Fisher could have become secure financially by devoting himself exclusively to American historical novels (as Harpers wanted him to do), but he had refused from the beginning to fit any category. He was at first considered a regionalist, then a sociological-psychological novelist, then a historical novelist. But Fisher was unhappy with the autobiographical novels and with his second marriage, which had disintegrated partly because of his wife's deep religious convictions. He felt that, if he could research deeply enough into the past, he could write some novels which would satisfactorily explain his autobiographical protagonist.

In 1939 he and Margaret were divorced. The next year he married Opal Laurel Holmes, endowed with the patience necessary for companionship with the tireless Fisher who wanted to explore new intellectual frontiers, to take an intellectual journey as difficult as Lewis and Clark had taken on another frontier. Freed from the demands of the Federal Writers' Project, Fisher settled with his new wife near Hagerman, Idaho, in the beautiful Thousand Springs Valley. They built themselves a home and farm buildings, reproducing incidentally a good part of the environment of the basin home which had brought young Vardis such nightmares.

There Fisher has devoted himself to reading and to writing books. When the way has been as hazardous as that Lewis and Clark found, he has, like them, gone doggedly on. Having been denied a Guggenheim fellowship on four occasions, a Newberry fellowship, and a Ford Foundation grant, he has become accustomed to making his own way, though midway through the *Testament* he experienced agonizing struggles with publishers. Three publishers eventually found the series a poor financial risk and dropped Fisher, and others were wary of taking over in the middle of a financially unsound series which was potentially explosive in its subject matter. Ironically Fisher expected controversy to make these volumes best-sellers. Fisher thought of himself as a writer for the "long pull" who would ultimately pay the publisher who stood by him. *Jesus Came Again* and the subsequent *Testament* volumes Fisher wrote seemed destined to be unpublished novels.

Fisher himself was at a loss about what to do, and he was sustained only by his vision of the work and by his wife's confidence. The future of the *Testament* brightened only when Alan Swallow, who is especially interested in *belles lettres* of the United States West, approached Fisher about letting his small firm bring out the novels—at a considerable gamble for Swallow, who was, however, absolutely convinced of Fisher's literary merit. The Fishers and Swallow worked tirelessly to get a subscription list of Fisher's friends to insure a chance of breaking even. Fisher had meanwhile kept himself going financially with the American historical novels that were always "extra" books for him and not, he felt, his major contribution.

With his disappointments from the response to his work, he has found new joys. He lives by a fairly regular routine, except when visitors are in the guest cabin where he and Opal first lived while building their permanent home. He writes in the morning and does hard labor on the farm in the afternoons. He has occasionally accepted invitations to lecture and participate in writers' conferences, but he has never felt comfortable in public assemblies. In the evenings he reads or drinks and talks with his wife and friends. He also enjoys great music—overtures, sonatas, concertos, arias, operas, symphonies. His inspiration comes from the scholarly books with which he surrounds himself and from the wilds of the nature around him. The Idaho terrain and Rocky Mountains have nourished Fisher's art from the first to last. Like his Mormon ancestors, Fisher has made the desert bloom. He has planted hundreds of trees and has himself put in an elaborate irrigating system from the spring that rushes down the hillside into the clear lake which his home overlooks. He loves hard labor—and despite failing sight and hearing, heavy drinking, and smoking—he looks quite robust.

Fisher and his wife have made three trips to Europe, and in 1956 they visited the Middle East as well. (Fisher had also spent the summer of 1930 in Europe). All of these trips were made with very little money in the autumn and early winter season since the Fishers cannot be away from their ranch in summer when they must irrigate their trees.

The pleasures of the middle and late years are quieter and reflect the more tolerant spirit Fisher has acquired—though life with him can still be highly emotional. His standards for intellectual honesty are as rigorous as ever, but his love seems greater, and he has usually expressed a profound sympathy for suffering. He is not bitter about his neglect, for his mail brings substantial numbers of intelligent letters from appreciative readers of the *Testament*. He notes with a twinkle in his eye that they are mainly from college-age students. Fisher usually talks about his career with an appropriate sense of humor.

Throughout the years his style has remained impassioned, for Fisher never feels at home on middle ground. His drive seems as undaunted as when he forced himself to develop physical prowess to protect his brother. Moreover, he is keenly aware of the world. For years he has published a political column in Idaho newspapers; and, in typical Fisher fashion, he has attacked popular views, earning for himself the title, "Old Irascible." From first to last, Fisher's frank statements have caused protest and neglect for his books. A less vigorous spirit would have buckled under the pressures of writing a historical series which no publisher wanted. The way for Fisher has not been an easy one, and there is something poetically appropriate in his not only beginning the historical pilgrimage but also living to finish it. Wherever one looks in Fisher, one finds the same drive, the same will to discover and to do.

CHAPTER *2*

Confession as Novel: Structure and Theme in the Vridar Hunter Tetralogy

NUMEROUS DISTINGUISHED NOVELS and stories of the twentieth century have used the artist as hero, and frequently the hero is a rather obvious mask for the writer. Proust, Joyce, and Wolfe are writ large on the list of such novelists. The twentieth-century autobiographical novelists continue the *Bildungsroman* tradition fathered by Goethe's *Wilhelm Meister*, the story of a young man's apprenticeship to life. In his famous essay on Freud and literature, Lionel Trilling declares that the *Bildungsroman* tradition had a profound effect on the revolution of morals which accompanied the Romantic movement. He cites at the same time as an important cause for the popularity of the tradition the fact that the novels give "almost complete identification of author and hero, and of the reader with both, and this identification almost inevitably suggests a leniency of moral judgment."[1] The reader, then, feels a "vested interest" in the hero's fortune.

Vardis Fisher's first substantial acclaim came with his autobiographical tetralogy: *In Tragic Life* (1932), *Passions Spin the Plot* (1934), *We Are Betrayed* (1935), *No Villain Need Be* (1936). An understanding of this work is a natural starting point for the understanding of the larger body of his fiction. The tetralogy provides the rationale for what Fisher tried to achieve in it and in later works. In a provocative essay, "A Trivial Excursion in Modesty," Fisher offers some valuable insights on his tetralogy as well as about autobiographical novels in general. The autobiographical novelist is often like the character "quoted" in Cabell's *Beyond Life* who talks to empty benches in an auditorium and seeks not applause but answers to riddles. Fisher spells out his riddles in the tetralogy and presents at least tentative answers.

In the same essay, Fisher expresses dissatisfaction with the results of his efforts. He had intended to write his tetralogy as early as 1925, but he had postponed the writing for several years because he wanted to approach his material with an appropriate ironic perspective. Fisher says he should have waited longer than he did: "I intended the four volumes about Vridar Hunter to be a comedy in the Meredithian sense—though I realize now that too often the humor is that of Swift rather than of the Comic Spirit. Because it was too often cruel rather than kindly, I know that the project should have been longer delayed."[2]

Perhaps Fisher was motivated to write the tetralogy when he did because of the appearance in 1929 of his friend Thomas Wolfe's *Look Homeward, Angel.* Certainly the kind of book Wolfe wrote influenced the autobiographical books Fisher wrote: Fisher tried to avoid what he felt were Wolfe's greatest faults. Although Fisher approved Wolfe's statement that one writes a book in order to forget it, he felt that Wolfe could not forget his book since he never understood the riddle of himself and kept writing the same story.[3]

Fisher also turned again to the story of Vridar Hunter, but he did so many years later and then because he felt he could now answer the riddle. He termed the tetralogy a "monumental wail" which failed to explain the man. "Those who attempt to find the man in the child," he concluded, "are unsuccessful because the man is not there. The man is in all the centuries of our past history."[4] In order to find the man, Fisher undertook his elaborate *Testament of Man* series. *Orphans in Gethsemane* ended the series, and there, Fisher felt, the autobiographical story of Vridar could be told adequately.

The arresting first telling of Vridar's story is a logical place to begin to understand Vardis Fisher. The tetralogy not only gave its author fame but consequently determined the course of his career. This chapter will analyze the qualities in Fisher's art which attracted attention and, with the following chapter on the revised version, explain the development of Fisher's philosophy of art and life.

I *"Ghost Come Back Again"*

Alan Swallow suggests that Vardis Fisher has not received his due because he is an intellectual novelist, a novelist in the tradition of Johnson's *Rasselas* and of Meredith—a tradition concerned primarily with idea and not presently popular.[5] The term "novel of ideas" had little currency before Aldous Huxley's *Point Counter Point* (1928). In *Point Counter Point* characters are interesting in large measure for the philosophy of life they hold and *talk out* in the novel. The hero, Philip Quarles, an uncommitted intellectual, enables the author to present many positions without affirming any, a technique well-suited to an age of intellectual confusion like the 1920's. As the title suggests, the play of ideas forms a kind of rhythmic composition.

However, the hero of the novel of ideas need not be like Philip Quarles. What the character comes to believe is not only a part of the characterization but may be as important as the characterization itself. The hero of Fisher's tetralogy talks a great deal about many things—books he has read, his notions of what a novelist should do, how one should live life. The reader who is impatient with talk about ideas will become very impatient with portions of the tetralogy, particularly in *No Villain Need Be* and with the second half of *Orphans in Gethsemane,* which is entitled *Ourania Aphrodite,* meaning intellectual or spiritual love. Consideration of the books about Vridar Hunter as novels of ideas is, therefore, necessary.

Fisher has long been attracted to the tradition of the novel of ideas. One of the nineteenth-century English novelists Vridar found most worth while was Thomas Love Peacock (the other two are Jane Austen and George Meredith) who developed the country-house discussion novel. In these novels characters gather to talk things over in a leisurely fashion. Plot hardly exists; but, when he can have mind and wit, Vridar is not one to complain about plot. Certainly plot is not a major strength of Vridar's favorite American novelist, James Branch Cabell.

The tradition of the *Bildungsroman,* also lends itself easily to discussions of ideas. The apprenticeship novel need not involve "intellectual" discussions, but it is likely to lead to them. D. H. Lawrence's *Sons and Lovers* (1913) is the story of Paul Morrell's preparation for life, but the characters never talk through intellectual problems; one does not think of Paul as living a life of the mind. However, W. Somerset Maugham's *Of Human Bondage* (1915) includes quite naturally philosophic discussions of art and what life is. James Joyce's *Portrait of the Artist as a Young*

Man (1916) has even more intellectual conversation. In fact, the last part of the book consists mainly of lengthy discussions of philosophy and esthetics and of arguments against Irish nationalism and the Roman Catholic Church, and it ends with the journal of the young intellectual. Vardis Fisher's tetralogy, but not his *Orphans in Gethsemane,* is the story of a preparation for life and writing, and it belongs in the tradition of the intellectual apprenticeship novel.

Reviewers generally found *No Villain Need Be* inferior to the other three novels of the tetralogy. It seemed to them not only too full of talk but looser in structure. They were, however, considering it as a novel by itself, and—though it cannot stand alone as easily as the other books of the tetralogy—when it is considered with them, it gains considerably in poignancy. Mark Van Doren and others decried the excess of autobiography at the end of the tetralogy, but, if the events are autobiographical, Fisher has selected them in keeping with his larger themes and in an attempt to bring all four novels together.

In fact, Fisher's tetralogy, like Huxley's novel, aspires to the condition of music. The four books follow the pattern of the conventional symphony. *In Tragic Life* states all of the themes that are recapitulated in the final book, *No Villain Need Be.* Fisher considered *Passions Spin the Plot* as the lyrical movement and *We Are Betrayed* as the scherzo. The division of the books into sections, an experiment with handling time, also suggests a musical analogy. No matter what one thinks of the value of Vridar's explanations of life, it is difficult to miss the heightened effect at the conclusion of *No Villain Need Be* where Vridar and Athene catalog the American experience to produce a coda.

The narrative technique of the tetralogy is more elaborate than the criticism which first labeled Fisher a Naturalist would indicate. The discourses of the last volume are anticipated in the musical structure of the whole, and they are also a logical result of the Naturalistic approach to the material defined in the novels' point of view.

As an apprenticeship novel, the tetralogy is concerned primarily with a single consciousness. The reader is occasionally reminded of the author's observation of the hero, but everything is seen from the viewpoint of the hero, Vridar Hunter; for the portrait

of the artist as a young man—very unlike Joyce's story of Stephen
Daedalus which is given as present time—is being told by the
hero who has completed his apprenticeship. From the beginning
of *In Tragic Life,* the reader is aware that the author is observing
his material from a vantage in time. But Vridar's story is not
unfolded in a successive series designed to place the reader in
the past and make him forget the present. Fisher's handling of
time is vitally related to the meaning of the tetralogy.

In Tragic Life is divided into three parts. Each is prefaced
by a shorter italicized section which bears a date: July 4, 1922;
October 17, 1930; September 10, 1929. The dates and italicized
passages set down specific moments of time which are clearly
different from that dealt with in the section. Each suggests that
the hero is looking back at an earlier time and is trying to come
to terms with it. The range of dates suggests that the answers
are not easily obtained and that mere chronological order will
not suffice. The dates chosen for *Passions Spin the Plot* are
March 17, 1926; May 16, 1931; December 31, 1929; June 17,
1923. Vridar is in his twenties on these days, but the novels
deal with him as a child and teen-ager. Novel time in *We Are
Betrayed* and in *No Villain Need Be* is the 1920's and 1930's,
when the hero is in his late twenties and early thirties. The
sections are prefaced with short passages that the reader has
already met in *In Tragic Life* and in *Passions Spin the Plot,*
and the early dates which apply are all days which were
important to Vridar as a young boy and teen-ager. Incorporated
into the last two books are passages which served as prefaces to
the first two books. Besides setting tone, foreshadowing events,
and suggesting theme in a particular section, the short prefaces
keep the reader mindful of the time perspective. The dates in
the first two books set a distance from which the events will
be viewed; the dates in the latter two books remind the
reader that the events of the past have shaped the present and
must be faced.

The method of discourse in the novels is also geared to keeping
the perspective of a searching of things past. Characteristic of the
narrative method of *In Tragic Life* is the following paragraph:

> Vridar was assured, again and again in a later time, that he
> was a remarkable child. He distrusted these tales, suspecting
> they were largely the seed and growth of a mother's wish, but

he always listened to them with a shrug of contempt. He was told that he talked at nine months, walked easily and well before his first birthday, and counted to a hundred at the age of two. At the age of three, he knew his multiplication tables to the sixes; at four he could add and subtract, at six he was reading the Bible. Of this dubiously precocious while he remembered little. Of his life, indeed, before the age of six he could recall only three experiences. They were all darkly significant; from each he reaped the whirlwind (32).[6]

Fisher then proceeds to relate the three earliest memories in order. These are followed by an account of the family's move to the desolate Antelope Hills and by Vridar's "earliest memories of blood and death" (46). Fisher presents each in a short episode; these episodes derive their unity from the themes that Vridar from a later time considered. He is obviously looking for order and patterns in his life. His later thoughts on an event are not interruptions since the whole technique is geared to analysis and to understanding of what has happened. Thus it is that the reader is always reminded of Vridar in a later time, of a Vridar who recognizes that he did something for *these* three or four reasons or *those* three reasons. All four novels are, therefore, a selection of remembered short scenes. Vridar, psychoanalyzing himself, selects moments which reveal his character and which give variations to the major themes. A part of the laboratory display of material is the presentation of a part of Vridar's early book, his letters, his journal, and his poems.

The narrative technique is, in part, protest against what Vridar feels to be the staple of autobiographical fiction: self-love. Of Proust, Vridar says, "In his huge volume he never once dug to the real important truth about himself" (*No Villain Need Be*, 177). Vridar decides to write a book that will be different. He attempts to write, though he knows it will not be possible, a completely honest book.

Just before Vridar writes his own autobiographical novel, his friend and colleague at New York University, Robert Clark, had finished his first novel. The personality behind Clark is Thomas Wolfe, and the novel is *Look Homeward, Angel*, as Fisher's articles on his friendship with Wolfe prove. Clark's book is described as:

a sprawling chaos of a book, a cyclone of power and rhetoric: it gathered sham and flummery to its tide and heaped the dishonest gestures into mountainous distortions. In its huge and hungry way, it had taken from a score of novelists, and from Clark himself, the best and the worst and transmuted these into a personality and a vision of its own. But in spite of its self-pitying rhapsodies, its self-induced and drunken apostrophizing of empire and destiny, it was, in Vridar's opinion, one of the greatest novels that had come out of American life (*No Villain Need Be*, 299).

The Robert Clark section comes immediately after a discussion about writers and critics by Vridar and Athene. Vridar says, "An honest book? It's not possible today to imagine, even to imagine vaguely, what an honest book, would be like" (*No Villain Need Be*, 298). The Clark discussion attempts to show that one of the most talented contemporary writers has fallen short because of his overwhelming desire for sympathy and self-glorification. Vridar, who recognizes at once that he and Clark had similar backgrounds and natures, wishes to avoid rhapsodies of self-love.

Fisher's insistence on distance and analysis is also a part of his attempt to avoid the sprawling effect of *Look Homeward, Angel* and to gain realism. Chapter Two of *In Tragic Life* enumerates Vridar's memories before age six, but they (like much in Fisher's book) invite comparison and contrast with the memories of Eugene Gant. Symbolic of the self-glorification to which Fisher objects is Chapter Four of *Look Homeward, Angel*, in which baby Eugene is endowed with very adult thoughts.[7] Fisher's method is closer to the way in which one must recapture those early years. Fisher also pokes a little fun at Wolfe by playing with Wolfe's adjective *wolfishly*. Vridar also reads wolfishly, but not to such an extent that he seems one of the greatest geniuses in the history of the race.

Fisher consciously rejects the kind of hero found in most novels. Near the end of *No Villain Need Be*, in a letter to his friend Telv, Vridar writes:

the vicarious urge today is so strong that if most critics read, let us say, a novel in which the hero is not glorified enough so they can identify themselves with him and in self-love fulfull his destiny, they are annoyed. They abuse him, and most likely they abuse the author too. This is not so if the "hero" belongs to poor white trash of the kind that critics patronizingly summarize as subhuman; but it is true if the protagonist is a person much like themselves who becomes "detestable" by revealing those traits which the critics themselves are trying to deny (351-52).

Much like the German dramatist Bertolt Brecht, Fisher seems to discourage identification with the hero. Brecht believes that identification brings catharsis; he wants rather to make his audience think. Thus it is with Fisher. He is purposely writing a *Bildungsroman* which does not have the identification which Trilling and Fisher found to be a trademark. When Vridar starts writing his novel at the end of *No Villain Need Be,* he often breaks into laughter; he thinks his book is "high comedy" and his hero is a very funny person. It is as "high comedy" that the book makes its appeal to the mind, for Vridar is bent on exposing his hero at every turn.

Athene, however, has the last word about the comedy label: "And haven't you said that there is neither comedy nor tragedy in life? These, you said, are only two points of view, two distortions. You've said it is distortion to make either the point of view and approach in a novel. To make great fun of your protagonist would be as stupid as to glorify him—as most persons do when they write of themselves. In fact, Vridar, making fun would be just an oblique form of self-glorification" (378).

Vridar agrees with Athene, and we can assume that the book Vridar writes about himself is neither comedy nor tragedy. Although the tetralogy has several very humorous episodes, few readers would class it as comedy. The titles from Meredith's sonnet suggest tragedy, and the portrait of Vridar and Neloa are too life-like for effective comedy. The protagonist in Vridar's book is to be shown for what he is: "a tragic and comic two-face:/hero and hoodlum: phantom and gorilla twist-/ing to moan with a gargoyle mouth," as Carl Sandburg has it in "The People, Yes."

Fisher sometimes allows his reader to sympathize with Vridar, but he never makes Vridar completely admirable. Vridar's apprenticeship ends, but he never achieves complete maturity. Typical of Fisher's exposure of his protagonist's immaturity is

Vridar's oral examination for his doctor's degree. When Vridar takes his degree, he is fighting through to a workable code of life, but at times he relies too strongly on the ironic muse. The committee asks Vridar to read *Beowulf*. Although he has nearly memorized the poem, he reads and translates badly. The sophomoric reasserts itself: "He wanted to crawl out on hands and knees and knock his head on a wall. I'm a fool, he thought desperately. Life isn't worth such humiliation. I'll give blow for blow" *(No Villain Need Be,* 78). He later leaves the examination room "reflecting that he needed more of this sort of thing: something to slap him around and wake him up" (79).

II   *A Schizoid Personality*

Vridar often seems so ridiculous and inconsistent because of what he thinks of as a split personality. His great battle in *In Tragic Life* (and also in *No Villain Need Be)* is to keep his sanity, not to lose touch with reality. Among the most memorable scenes of the novel are those in which Vridar hears the buzzing of flies and feels his sanity weaken. He tries to break the heavy spell and to establish connections with reality by repeating words. Analyzing himself later, Vridar concludes that the tendency to insanity resulted from a split in his personality, and Fisher uses Vridar's explanation for literary purposes. The tetralogy is the story of Vridar's attempts to reconcile what he considers the two sides of his being. When he can come to terms with both, he has served his apprenticeship, and he can be a writer. The tetralogy gives increased emphasis to the dual personality theme, which is explained finally by reference to Vridar's brother's psychological theory of auto-correctivism.

Vridar, the amateur but often successful psychologist of *No Villain Need Be,* makes frequent mention of his brother's theory in his analyses. Vivian Fisher, Vardis' brother, defines the theory in his book *Auto-correctivism: The Psychology of Nervousness* (1937). Actually, Vivian's book had not appeared at the time Vardis was writing his tetralogy, but Vivian had been talking it through at the time, as Vardis has acknowledged.[8] Fisher also said that his brother's theory came largely from Jung. Whatever its source, the point is that the theory is given an important place in the scheme of the tetralogy. Very briefly, it states that the

individual is being pulled in two directions: by the demands
of the selfless or racial drives and by those of the selfish or ego
drives. The healthy individual has learned to balance these
conflicting drives, but if either end of the balance is heavier,
the individual will react "auto-correctively" to offset the pre-
dominant interest. The neurotic's symptom, therefore, is corrective
and prevents further imbalance.[9]

Vivian's theory struck his brother as one of the most meaningful explanations of the turmoil of the modern world, and Vardis
made frequent use of it in essays as well as in novels. Besides
resting his tetralogy on the theory, he wrote another novel shortly
afterward to illustrate it, *Forgive Us Our Virtues: A Comedy of
Evasions* (1938). This unusual novel is also in large part autobiographical, though these elements are more concealed than in
the tetralogy; and Fisher later incorporated parts of the theory
into *Orphans. Forgive Us Our Virtues* is not on a par with the
tetralogy, and Fisher wrote "it is not a novel, really but an
experiment and a failure: in the first three parts I condensed
three novels I had written that no publisher wanted."[10] The
comedy presents a series of psychological studies of persons
who are out of balance because of overemphasis on either ego
or racial drives. In the final section of the novel, Ogden Greb
has achieved something of a balanced personality. *Forgive Us
Our Virtues* is Fisher's attempt, therefore, to say in a more comic
vein the same thing he says in the tetralogy.

In Tragic Life indicates the forces which make Vridar's personality dangerously imbalanced. He has more than ordinary ego.
Humiliation, loneliness, and fear combine to make him abnor-
mally proud. From his earliest years he was unwilling to admit
defeat and preferred death to failure. He faced school bullies on
sheer grit, a pattern he was to follow through life. But Vridar
was never free to follow his egoistic drives, for his racial drives
were just as extreme. He wished to save the world, to become
a mighty force for good, and at one time he thinks God has called
him to be another Joseph Smith. Indeed, internal debate over
the reasons for becoming a Mormon missionary precipitates his
great crisis over masturbation. His sense of guilt over this practice
has been extreme and leads him to periodic insanity. In an
important scene near the end of *In Tragic Life* Fisher underscores
the division in Vridar and anticipates future consideration of

him in terms of the duality. The sixteen-year-old youth has been working on a neighboring farm. He enters into a spell of insanity, runs from the field into the house:

> Now he suffered a peculiar change. He stopped babbling now and peered, and his manner was sly and stealthy, as if another being possessed him. In reality, he was now two; the cowering terrified one and the crafty fascinated one. This crafty one wanted to look at the mirror and see his face. It drew him against all his will and he came on tiptoe and with held breath; and he glanced around, as if to see his foes; and he stopped a little, in an absurd way, as if the mirror would flee. He looked in. He stared for several moments. And what he saw was so ghastly in its whiteness, so wild and horrified and insane in its eyes, that he began to shake. Only in asylums, in a later time, did he ever see such a face as this. But he stared. He put his face close, drawn to those eyes, to the haunted tragic madness of those eyes.
>
> Then he swung, like a jungle thing, and raced outside and homeward, with a gathering of terror at his flying heels (393-94).

At high school his "ruthless personality" forces his "timid personality" to permit him to go to the school dances: "One part of him, really was thinking of excuses, preparing for failure; and the other part, stern and unpitying, whipped him to courage. 'You got to dance!' cried this stern part. 'Yes, yes,' said the other, in meek abasement, and hoped there would be no dance" (429).

The same forces debate in Vridar in *Passions Spin the Plot.* He goes to college dances after much the same battle. Fisher keeps the two-personality theme before the reader by both direction and indirection. When Vridar is going on his unreasoned crusade to defend Neloa's honor, the distant voice says, "So divorced, during this while, were two personalities within him that the one hardly knew what the other did. The one was sunk in weariness but the other still plotted" (401). At the core of Vridar's relationship with Neloa (about which the tetralogy revolves) is the split personality. Of Vridar's return to Neloa after he has tried to forget her, the author from his distance of years summarizes:

> And it may seem strange that Vridar, looking so unerringly into years ahead, did not pause now. In later years, indeed, it seemed strange to him. But his love for Neloa was so wildly

unreasoning, so much a part of his life and his loneliness, and so completely a pattern of his vanity and pride, that he had no power to renounce it. When far from her he could mark the danger zones. Then he could feel, however obscurely, that his hunger for achievement was not a part of her life; and that they would live as strangers in the same house. But when with her, or after thinking of her for a long while, she became for him, not the woman who had loved freely, but the shy lass on the Annis butte, the girl who had stood with him in the school contest, the terribly sweet thing, the symbol, the idea, that had been the core of his worship, the beat of his heart. To have forgotten her, or to have made her seem to him what she actually was, he would have to sever ten years of his life (356).

Fisher plays on the same chord in *We Are Betrayed*. The ex-fraternity member Vridar reacts dually to the scorn of his ex-brothers. One part is bewildered and aches for recognition. The other ruthlessly accepts the price of his convictions. The author from his distance again summarizes the conflict and reaffirms the basis for the rest of the action of the tetralogy:

> His idealism fought against his ruthless cunning, and their feud was so ceaseless, so implacable, that it gave him no peace. It split him into two personalities; and each of these was to grow and to become an almost undefeatable thing; until in this year, and more deeply in years lying ahead, he was to hang between two crosses, the one of life and the other of hate. He stood now, and he was to stand for a long time, between courage and fear, reaching to the one, trying to destroy the other. And his pilgrimage now became chiefly this struggle: to conquer fear and to rise to an unimpeachable integrity of heart and mind, and to lose his hatred in a love for all things (38-39).

Vridar's "pilgrimage"—a key word of the tetralogy (particularly in *We Are Betrayed*) which underscores the apprenticeship motif—involves a conflict between these two forces which often seems incapable of resolution. The battle between them becomes more severe. And with his personal life at odds, Vridar is unable to write anything that satisfies him. He notes in his journal: "My novel is pretty damned bad: I mix the simple and sardonic and get a broth of acid that simmers. On one Sunday the simpleton in me writes; on the next, the Jonathan Swift" *(We Are Betrayed*, 286).

But if Vridar is more unintegrated than ever after his search-
ings into literature, philosophy, and religion, he has at least
become aware of what his problem is. He tells Athene shortly
after he meets her:

> You ought to realize at once that there are two quite distinct
> personalities in me. Let's call them X and Y. X is credulous;
> believes in human beings; seeks only what he calls the beautiful
> and the good.
>
> Y is an ironic realist. He knows what human beings are like
> and looks at them in the detached spirit of the scientist. X sees
> the earth peopled with fallen saints, struggling heroically to
> regain their heaven. Y sees a vast spawn of apes with the jungle
> in their hearts. For X human beings are generous and warm-
> hearted; for Y they are more ferocious than the tiger and more
> venomous than the snake . . . (*We Are Betrayed*, 320).

Vridar tells Athene that he wants to become all Y, which,
according to the theory of auto-correctivism, is not possible; and,
of course, Vridar is highly unsuccessful. He continues to be X at
one moment and Y at another. Y cannot crush X, and Vridar is
not able to integrate them; indeed, he has not thought integra-
tion possible.

Neloa, who has suffered with often superhuman patience the
struggle between X and Y, becomes the victim of it. Her suicide,
however, makes possible Vridar's coming to terms with X and
Y. His whole treatment of Neloa in the catastrophe at the end
of *We Are Betrayed* exposes how empty has been so much of
his talk. He has mouthed honesty and integrity, but the man
who faces Neloa is the same blind "X" she faced in the Antelope
Hills. When Vridar is actually about to lose Neloa, X pushes
aside the ironic Y. Although intellectually Vridar has learned
some things about himself, emotionally he has learned little,
which is to say that X and Y are unintegrated.

After Neloa's suicide Vridar is, for a time, certain of nothing.
He is periodically insane and suicidal. But Fisher has shown the
determined ancestry from which Vridar comes, and Vridar has
repeatedly shown how strong his will to conquer is. The Y of
him, shut out largely by the catastrophe, reasserts its rights
when Vridar reads the analysis of himself in his brother Mertyl's
journal. He resolves then to face himself, to go back to his past

and become his own best psychologist. *No Villain Need Be* thematically completes Vridar Hunter's apprenticeship with his successful probings into his own nature.

III   *A Search For Meaning*

The ground that Vridar must cover is, of course, that of the first three volumes of the tetralogy. Fisher judges the excellence of a title on how well it suggests the meaning of the novel; in fact, the title is part of the novel.[11] The titles of the tetralogy come from one of Meredith's "sonnets" from *Modern Love* and are together thematically appropriate since Fisher, like Meredith, is reviewing and analyzing a tragic love experience. Meredith's memorable lines from Sonnet XLIII reveal the husband's mature insights after he has conquered the cynicism in which he first took refuge:

> 'Tis morning: but no morning can restore
> What we have forfeited. I see no sin:
> The wrong is mixed. In tragic life, God wot,
> No villain need be! Passions spin the plot:
> We are betrayed by what is false within.

Not only are the lines in keeping with Fisher's conclusion, but they also provide excellent titles for the individual books of the tetralogy, suggesting the meaning of each as well as unifying the totality. The titles of the first three books help catch the truths which Vridar, forced to look back after Neloa's suicide, finds.

In Tragic Life establishes the essential character traits that make Vridar Hunter's life tragic for at least thirty years—tragic in the sense of wasted or unfulfilled, as in Meredith's sonnet, rather than in the classical sense. The novel concludes by echoing a part of a line from the same Meredith passage from which all of the titles are taken: "I see no sin." Tragedy is not a matter of sin but of the heritage of the individual. Turner, Vridar's favorite high school teacher, strikes another Meredithian note when he explains to Vridar that the only sin is in rejecting life: "The only religion lay in accepting life honestly and strongly" (462). *In Tragic Life* sets forth the reasons for Vridar's being able to realize Turner's religion only after fierce struggle.

The title *Passions Spin the Plot* suits admirably the story of Vridar and Neloa's courtship to their marriage. It captures the sense of foreboding on which the novel ends. The tragedy of the marriage, which is sometimes amusingly and bitterly foreshadowed—as when Vridar reads *Jude the Obscure* or reflects that he will not be an Angel Clare nor Neloa a Tess—seems inevitable when the novel ends. The title, too, indicates the coming tragedy. Passions, the X of Vridar, have led to the fatal marriage. Vridar, so controlled by his romantic demon, is incapable of Turner's joy.

We Are Betrayed takes the reader to the catastrophe. The betrayal is not only Vridar's and Neloa's but the nation's as well. Oscar Cargill complains that Vridar Hunter's story is too unique and without universal application,[12] but Fisher has carefully prepared the reader for seeing Vridar's story as an American one with important implications. *We Are Betrayed* takes Vridar into the United States Army and finally from the West to Chicago, and it focuses his story more sharply as an American tragedy. The novel time of *We Are Betrayed* is that of World War I and the post-war years. The sense of national betrayal which many Americans felt after the war becomes the background for Vridar's personal tragedy. His pilgrimage takes him to the heart of the decade, and *We Are Betrayed* is in part a record of that period.

Through inspection of his own life, Vridar later comes to feel that he understands the national and the racial betrayal. *No Villain Need Be* "talks out" the forces which have made of Vridar's life such great sorrow. An emotional understanding of the causes of betrayal finally leads him to assert that no villain need be; that is, life need not be tragic if man will, as Turner at the end of *In Tragic Life* said he should, accept what he is with emotional honesty. Facing squarely what he is and what the race is leads Vridar to his great affirmation: "When we look back upon that long lone way of darkness, upon that magnificent heritage and birthright of our race, then we feel the humility, the awe, the pride in which is to be found our noble and mighty strength. In all that lies our certain knowledge that no villain need be. Out of all that, once we sense it deeply, will come a splendid fellowship, and fellowship when it comes will be enough..." (389).

IV *Sources of Betrayal*

What are the things which Vridar finds have betrayed him and America when he looks back at his heritage? In *No Villain Need Be* he repeatedly says that Puritanism is responsible for the betrayals and evasions of America. But Puritanism only suggests what Vridar objects to. He tries to make of Prudence an American symbol for what he means: "My mother represents one way of life that is the heart and core of this wretched country we live in" (151).

Prudence is herself a "betrayed" creature, and in only a very superficial sense can she be viewed as villain. She is a part of a larger theme of the tetralogy: the "woman problem." She teaches Vridar that women are, unless corrupted by men, noble and virtuous. Although Cabell offers Vridar insights into women, Vridar is unable to overthrow his mother's teachings; and it is only after Neloa's death that he understands women. Emotionally, Vridar clings to notions of good and evil. Sex is something that disturbs his world, for it is aligned with pleasure rather than duty, and in Prudence's manner Vridar distrusts pleasure. Vridar's concept of women betrays him to the colossal stupidities which are the stuff and substance of the tetralogy.

Almost as important and almost as central to Vridar's tragedy as the betrayal at his mother's knee is the betrayal by books. As a young boy Vridar read avidly, and most of what he read confirmed the teachings of his mother. Much of his early reading was in the Bible of which the Hunters had two: a children's Bible and another with small print. In the Bible with small print Vridar found some disturbing things, and Prudence concealed the truth when Vridar asked her questions about them. From his Bible reading, however, came a huge desire to be a great prophet of God. From other books in the Hunter house, Vridar learned to identify himself with heroes like Kit Carson and Daniel Boone. He developed a strong desire to dramatize his life, to make of himself a noble hero. Sentimental novels, such as those by Mrs. Southworth or Bertha M. Clay, filled the loneliness of the Antelope hours, but they also confirmed the false teachings of his mother. They showed life as a matter of heroes and villains, of good and bad. In this vein Vridar writes in high school his first novel, significantly titled *A Man among Villains.*

In the post-war rioting, Vridar starts his first real study of human character. As he associates with pimps, prostitutes, and bootleggers, he begins to understand human nature. He tells Neloa, "I always thought there were good people and bad people. In books they're that way. In books it's villains and heroes" *(We Are Betrayed,* 118). *Passions Spin the Plot* had illustrated how ridiculous Vridar's beliefs in villains had made him. In *We Are Betrayed* Vridar senses that he himself will never write worthwhile books as long as he knows so little of human nature. His search also becomes one for a code of life which will make him a writer. He does write when he returns to school, but his work reveals how far he is from a workable code: "His allegory would be a pattern so rich and deep with color that he would see no meaning, no coherence, in the heaped voluptuous masses of his effort; and feel only intoxication and chaos, as when he stared at the formless glories of a sunset" (154). He resolves, nevertheless, to dedicate his life to art; and, during the time he is torn between Athene and Neloa, he sees himself as another Shelley, which also indicates how far he is from the code he seeks.

Later when Vridar is well along the way to being an integrated personality, he is able to recommend only a few modern American novelists who seem to understand human nature and to have something to say: Cabell, Robert Nathan, Ellen Glasgow. As he sees through himself, Vridar becomes in *No Villain Need Be* increasingly better equipped to write books which will ring true about life. The morbid introvert of the first three books was essentially incapable of knowing how others feel, but he begins to acquire this ability in *We Are Betrayed,* and the reader can measure Vridar's growth in his understanding and feeling for others. *No Villain Need Be* portrays him with a heightened sense of reality and as gathering important insights for writing.

As an author Vridar wants his books to give to other Vridars the direction that he failed to find in literature. A significant portion of the tetralogy deals with Vridar as student and teacher. As a teacher he also wants to give the kind of leadership he failed to find, for this, too, is another source of his betrayal. His elementary school training is brutal and more typical of frontier America. However, his high school training anticipates a larger concern with American education. Vridar goes to high school in Rigby looking for wisdom and direction, but he finds it to be mean, the students uninterested in learning, and the teachers neurotic and ineffective. Only later does Vridar realize the significance of the politics and evasions of his high school.

The education theme, only lightly touched in *In Tragic Life*, becomes major in the other three novels. As a college freshman in *Passions Spin the Plot*, Vridar is more zealous for truth than most, but he is gradually forced to conclude that the students and faculty at Wasatch College were not interested in truth. Education turned out to be one more empty faith. Partly because of his keen disappointment, Vridar decides during his shattering freshman year that he will dedicate his life to honest and courageous teaching.

Vridar is, of course, a very odd character in college. Eugene Gant, also an odd one, was able to find some fellowship and purpose in school life, but Vridar is completely off to the side. His first two years are filled with rowdyism and tortures over sex. After he marries Neloa, he plays on the college football team and joins a fraternity. Football and fraternity life are college for most of the students on the Wasatch campus, but Vridar is as isolated as ever.

When Vridar starts graduate studies at Midwestern University, he has an intimation of what a university should be. But his own teaching experience at Wasatch indicates why the relatively high standards of Midwestern are not more widely prevalent. Vridar as a teacher becomes even more aware that many of the faculty are evasive persons who are unable to face the truth about themselves. Many are overly concerned with petty school squabbles and school politics. But what about the teachers who are honestly trying to give their students intellectual leadership?

Vridar's teaching career at Wasatch College suggests the answer to the problem. Vridar defines the teacher's purpose and duty as follows: "to arouse my students to an intelligent and alert interest in contemporary affairs and thought; to awaken them to the possibilities of their own minds; and to suggest to them the stupidity of believing in anything merely because it is the belief of someone else. I try to persuade them to think, not as I think, not as you or anyone else thinks, but as they must honestly think after they have examined the evidence" *(No Villain*

Need Be, 90). Following this code brings the young instructor trouble and grief. Students complain, misquote him, and parents write letters to the president objecting to the atheistic instructor. The president is trying to do a good job, but he is bound by the narrow Mormon community whose servant he is. Vridar learns from all this that American public schools can only be as good as the citizens will let them. Merely criticizing professors and administrators only gets to the surface of the problem. The source of the trouble is in all of the romantic evasions which are ingrained in the nation.

The education issue, quite obviously, helps Fisher to broaden the scope of the tetralogy's meaning from simply a personal story to an "American" one. Finally Vridar's pilgrimage is a symbol of the pilgrimage of his nation and race. His disappointment in the education at Wasatch coupled with that over the start of World War I make him more conscious of his country, of what it means and of where it is going. The social theme is anticipated in *In Tragic Life* when high schooler Vridar becomes the enraged idealist and resolves to write on social themes. The high school boy's novel does just that, but his social passions stem largely from his own feelings of inferiority and self-pity. In *Passions Spin the Plot* he is more honestly searching for answers to social problems. When the United States enters the war, the campus is caught in a wave of patriotism; but Vridar feels betrayed.

The title *We Are Betrayed* captures the larger sense of betrayal that the nation as a whole felt after the war. Vridar's war experiences expose how empty most of the slogans were. As an enlistee in the air force, Vridar finds an aristocratic system which denies the principle of a world safe for democracy. As a draftee in the army, he finds, as he suspected, that war involved primarily the development of jungle instincts. When he leaves the service at the Armistice, he is a victim of the post-war frustration; and, like many others, he turns for a while to a life of bootlegging and drink. He moves on the fringe of the underworld of little Idaho Falls. Later in Chicago he contemplates a life of crime, for he finally finds honesty even though among thieves.

Vridar's discussions about America in *We Are Betrayed* and in *No Villain Need Be* show how most of the specifics of Frederick Lewis Allen's *Only Yesterday* affect a sensitive young man of the period. Vridar's disillusionment sends him, as it sent many intellectuals who were disillusioned by the American scene, to a consideration of communism. One of his journal items says: "Am reading Marx: he was a great and noble man. Communism, as employed in Russia, is possibly, it seems to me, the nearest approach yet made to the teachings of the Christ; and for that reason, of course, is anathema to 'Christians' quite as Spinoza, great and noble fellow, was to the Jews. Except for the faint light of Marx, I've found nothing yet in books to sustain me..." (*We Are Betrayed*, 287).

Fisher portrays, too, the uncertain intellectuals at gin parties, who know all about Freud and the new psychology but are nevertheless part of the "lost generation." Later Vridar and Athene journey to Europe, and the trip provides Vridar with the opportunity to view his country from a new perspective, to understand America's vulgarities in relation to the rest of Western civilization.

V   *Program for Reform*

Vridar, symbol of the American neurosis everywhere apparent, satisfactorily concludes his pilgrimage and arrives at his affirmation that "no villain need be." The aspiring young writer is finally able to face his art with confidence. How he achieves this confidence is the substance of most of the discussions of *No Villain Need Be*, the concluding book of the tetralogy, which attempts to answer the old question, "What must I do to be saved?" Vridar presents the answer in terms of auto-correctivism and the integrated personality. As we have seen, the seeker must pitilessly explore his past to discover his evasions. But most evasions are so deeply buried that discovery is not easy. Vridar uncovers his evasions not only through long looks at his own childhood, but through careful study of his dreams. He measures his progress in self-discovery by his increasing tendency to more literal dreams. Two other aids to a frank confrontation are drink and sex. Alcohol, Vridar says, should be an "instrument of courage and strength" (248). Drink can be for the intelligent an instrument of catharsis.

The intelligent person can also use sex as an instrument of catharsis. Because of a heritage of false ideals, most persons, Vridar feels, are obsessed with sex. The sex motive is essentially a race motive, but for most it is unclean. Vridar has been sexually neurotic from earliest years, and artistic honesty demands that he come to terms with the problem in *No Villain Need Be*. There he tells Athene, "I'll not be another D. H. Lawrence, trying desperately in one book after another to arrive at a decent copulation" (234). Consequently, he goes, without Athene, to Salt Lake City to try to come to terms with his obsessions with sex. The return to the capital of Mormondom is, of course, a return to the scene of his youthful frustrations and longing for sexual fulfillment. When in college, he had been unable to be sexually intimate with women; he now returns to have several sexual affairs with former students and other women. He learns, he tells Athene later, that in all the time since Neloa's death he has still been seeking her. The summer's experiences, though not so well created as the desires in the earlier books, indicate that Vridar has counteracted his earlier imbalance.

Vridar's reference to D. H. Lawrence is not beside the point. The whole problem of evasions in our Western heritage, as Vridar sees it, takes its focus in the problem of the relationship between the sexes; and the problem takes its most cogent form, in the tetralogy, in the person of Neloa. From the beginning, there was something in Neloa which Vridar could not understand. He sees something in her eyes which he is unable to fathom; and, because he is so certain of what Neloa should be, he fails to look more deeply. He makes of her an ideal; she represented all of the things which life had denied him; and she was all that was holy. When Vridar discovers something which does not conform to his image of her, he resolves to shape her to that image. And though a young man of nineteen, he is not even aware of desiring Neloa sexually.

Neloa, however, primitive and passionate as she is, does not wish to be a symbol. Because she is so unashamedly female, she is puzzling to Vridar. One of the experiences which interrupted his idyllic courtship was his unexpected visit to Neloa on the Mormon holiday. When Neloa saw Vridar come, she ran into the house and pretended to be asleep. When she denies having done so, Vridar is outraged and wants to know why she lied. The event is a trifle, but an important one; it not only exposes Vridar but suggests the deeper side of Neloa. She seems to have acted from a desire to make something more of Vridar than a worshiper at a shrine: she desires to be treated as a woman. Her disobedience to his wishes when she danced with others, after having promised not to, stems from her desire to force Vridar into a new kind of relationship with her. But Vridar does not understand. He frequently notes the scorn in her eyes, but he does not recognize that she is scornful because he will not realize that she is female waiting for the male.

After Neloa's suicide, Vridar comes to understand that her way was pagan, clean, good; but he, aware of the split in his own personality, earlier had made a duality of Neloa. Vridar's destruction of Neloa is symbolized in Vridar's morbid activities before his marriage. He takes Neloa to a grove and forces her to pose for two photos. In one he wants the prostitute, in the other the angel: Moll and Mifanwy. His aim is to destroy Moll and make Neloa all Mifanwy. He repeatedly wonders which of the two he has married. Neloa, of course, tries to be Mifanwy; but this role denies her true womanly nature. The duality in Neloa is largely one Vridar has imposed upon her, much as—Vridar comes to feel—Western man has everywhere denied to women an honest fulfillment of their being, just as Vridar's mother had been denied. Vridar realizes after his own tragedy that the right man could have made Prudence realize her womanhood. Instead, Prudence becomes a fierce embodiment of the repressive way of life that is betraying her sex.

Vridar's coming to terms with sex is largely presented—despite the chapter of his visit to Salt Lake City—through discussions, and, in fact, D. H. Lawrence is mentioned several times in these discussions. Vridar's analysis of *Lady Chatterley's Lover,* a prohibited book Vridar smuggles into America on his return from Europe, is thematically to the point of the tetralogy. He writes in his journal: "It is a sincere story and in some respects an important one. All his life Lawrence struggled to write one book, and from the groping *Sons and Lovers* to this last effort, he made an agonizingly slow pilgrimage to an idea, a vision, which he never emotionally came to. Only intellectually did he achieve it. He understood what we must all understand: that we can never be reasonable as long as the mind is ashamed of the body, the body afraid of the mind" (*No Villain Need Be,* 341).

Vridar objects to some of Lawrence's conclusions, doubts that Lawrence saw his own self-love, or how traditions established the disharmony of the modern world; but he thinks his basic point of the need for the balance between mind and body crucial. For he had once been a Lady Chatterley, ashamed and humiliated by his body. Like the stupid and ridiculous John Smith of *Forgive Us Our Virtues*, whose name suggests an American Everyman, Vridar disguised his stupidities and evasions as virtues. John and Vridar both assert violently and repeatedly that they are being completely honest. Those who understand must forgive their virtues, which in reality are evasions.

To integrate his personality, Vridar has used, then, not only a painstaking analysis of his past and dreams but a conscious use of liquor and sex to break down his own established notions. He has balanced the X and Y of his personality, the racial and the egoistical; thus he is able to chart his course for the future. But still partly an idealist, he hopes to aid the race to a new realization of itself. He feels he has a firm basis for his own life and is now able to dedicate his life to writing. Symbolic of the fact that he has served his apprenticeship is section four of *No Villain Need Be*, in which he returns to his Antelope homeland. The casual reader of *We Are Betrayed* may be puzzled by Fisher's inclusion of a short chapter, dramatically unsatisfying, in which Vridar and Neloa leave Chicago to spend a summer in Idaho, ostensibly to save money. In the scheme of the tetralogy, the chapter, which shows a frustrated Vridar fighting with his parents and re-reading the Bible, has a symbolic meaning. The tetralogy is the story of Vridar's coming to terms with his past, his homeland. He feels his return with Neloa is a mistake, for he still hates the Antelope country. His return in *No Villain Need Be* symbolizes his success in unifying the disparate sides of his nature, which had taken such extreme form in that frontier outpost. The plot has come full cycle. The joy which Vridar desires at the end of *In Tragic Life* and which he has come to learn is the rightful possession of human beings is at last his.

In a lecture in 1953, Fisher said: "As I see it, the chief task of the novelist is sufficiently to liberate himself from his background to be able to see it in some kind of perspective. . . . We have in some manner to break free, without on the one hand losing touch with the stuff that made us, without on the other mistaking our self-protective illusions for truth."[13] When the tetralogy ends, Vridar has liberated himself and is ready to write.

CHAPTER 3

Experience Refocused: Structure and Theme in *Orphans in Gethsemane*

FISHER'S TETRALOGY understandably made him a known writer in the 1930's. But by writing a *Bildungsroman* in which the reader was not invited to identify with the hero, Fisher assumed great risks, and many critics turned from him in anger as the tetralogy concluded. Most of them admitted, however, that there was great power in much of Vridar's story; and, indeed, the whole has much more artistic integrity than many of the critics were able to see as they read the books volume by volume rather than as a single work. The books were certainly not a staple of Naturalistic fiction.

Nevertheless, the work is uneven, and the final volume is most certainly inferior dramatically. Fisher's revision and extension of the tetralogy as the last volume of his *Testament of Man* series did not remove every blemish, but *Orphans in Gethsemane* does present a more significant Vridar story. In *Orphans* one sees that Fisher has become a more profound thinker and has written a more satisfying autobiographical novel. In it he spells out the philosophy of the mature Fisher, and therefore we will consider the new Vridar story in juxtaposition to the tetralogy rather than at the conclusion of our consideration of the *Testament,* though some references to the *Testament* are, of course, necessary.

I *A Novel of the Past in the Present*

As we have noted, Fisher said that his sense of failure with the tetralogy grew greater with the years. He declared that exploring a man's childhood was not sufficient for explaining the man that came to be.[1] Fred T. Marsh seems to have anticipated

Fisher's objection in his essentially sympathetic review of *No Villain Need Be*. Marsh says that Vridar's new faith is not real enough, that the reader is not likely to believe in Vridar's solution, and that the ending is artificial.[2] Fisher also agrees that the fourth novel was the weakest. Not surprisingly, it is the part of the tetralogy most radically revised in *Orphans*. In his short preface to *Orphans* Fisher says, "I suspect that it was Vridar who went to pieces: imagining that he had become adult, he mistook a light for an illumination" (5).

Orphans in Gethsemane, far from being an apprenticeship novel, rests upon eleven other novels and is offered as "a novel of the past in the present." It can briefly be described as the story of the man who wrote the *Testament of Man*, why he wrote it, and what conclusions he draws from it. A novel of ideas, it caps the researches behind many novels.

In order to avoid confusion, Fisher drops the Meredithian frame which so ably served the tetralogy. This change is thematically appropriate since Vridar's story no longer has as its core the tragic love affair with Neloa and Vridar's analysis of it. In general, however, the four books are structural units of *Orphans*, but are renamed for important myths. Fisher divides Vridar's life into two segments, divided by Neloa's suicide. Hence, Book I: *Aphrodite Pandamos* (Sensual Love of Body) corresponds in its three parts to the first three books of the tetralogy. Part one of Book II: *Ourania Aphrodite* (Intellectual Love of Mind) corresponds roughly with *No Villain Need Be*. Two other parts follow: one dealing mainly with Vridar's work with the Federal Writers' Project and the other with the researches for and the writing of the historical series.

The segments which correspond to the books of the tetralogy are presented, however, in new perspective. Whereas the individual novels of the tetralogy are in prefaced parts bearing dates to set a distance in time, *Orphans* moves in a more straightforward manner, much as the other novels in the *Testament of Man*. Fisher keeps some references about the Vridar of the future, though they are greatly reduced; moreover, they are more in the manner of the author's commenting directly—as he does in the other novels of the *Testament*—than in the manner of the self-probing from a distance as in the tetralogy. Omitted from *Orphans* are the analytical summaries and transitions. Vridar's journal is mostly integrated into the action, and the number of letters is greatly reduced—all of which tends to increase the sense of a story moving forward in time rather than of a psycho-analyst's case study. *Orphans* is also set up on paper to present a more continuous effect to the eye: the tetralogy's chapters are broken into segments; *Orphans* tries to unite these as it does chapters. The new novel is not divided into the four parts of the symphony, but Fisher still strives for effects of musical movements in the different sections. In the opening chapter of each book, he strikes the themes he will present in it, frequently using quotations to do so.

Whereas the tetralogy attempted to show how an American writer equipped himself for life and his craft and to account for that apprenticeship in terms of self-psychoanalysis and his childhood, *Orphans* attempts to show the present state of Western man and to account for it in terms of the race's past. In the tetralogy Vridar is an American symbol whose larger Occidental meaning is but suggested; in *Orphans* he is American more incidentally and is primarily a product of the Judaic-Christian heritage. He comes, moreover, to realize that he is such, a realization that Fisher thinks necessary if the race is to be truly civilized but which the Western world has not sufficiently grasped.

That Vridar is going to make more sweeping statements in *Orphans* and that his concern is going to be finally more with the race than himself are made clear in the *Iphigenia and Orestes (In Tragic Life)* section. After watching Joe and Nephi dehorn, brand, and castrate cattle, Vridar goes away sick. Fisher adds a paragraph not found in *In Tragic Life:*

> So these were men! These were men who believed in the gentle Jesus and all the Christian dogmas, who waged war on one another, who sawed and cut and burned until the poor creatures could no longer even bawl but were half-dead; these were men who did these things with no more emotion than they might feel when lighting their pipes or lacing their shoes! But what kind of men were these and what kind of thing was man? (*Orphans*, 122-23).

Vridar's great vow in *Orphans* is not just to find joy, to laugh, but more importantly to be a great scholar, to trace the Christian dogmas to their sources, to help the race build something more solid and certain. Whereas in the tetralogy Vridar is preparing to be a writer, in *Orphans* his wanting to write is more incidental to a wish for a long exploration into the past to understand why the present is as it is.

II *Major Changes*

To keep the new thread going, Fisher makes several changes from the tetralogy. One change is to give a more definite stress on the impact of the Bible on the Hunter home. For example, in *Orphans*, but not in *In Tragic Life*, Vridar's wise high school teacher, Turner, asks: "What have you read most in your life?" When Vridar tells him the Bible, Turner says, "Good God, that explains it" (219). And Vridar, fighting through the crisis after Neloa's suicide, reflects in *Orphans*: "The Bible and his mother had made an emotional imbecile of him" (552).

Another change is to make Vridar more intellectual and aware of his vow to be a scholar. In *Passions Spin the Plot* Vridar had been too busy to do much extra reading, but he reads widely in *Orphans* and begins at the same time to study photographs of apes and to search for the simian in the faces of his professors. These changes make the discussion of ideas become important sooner in *Orphans*. It is a naïve and lonely Vridar in *Passions Spin the Plot* who at the end of three weeks says to his roommate, Stanley Trout, "Isn't it wonderful! Being in college, I mean" (31). In *Orphans* at the same point he is reading a book by Edward Carpenter on the Catholic religion and tries to talk to Stanley about the nature of all religion (230). Periodically Vridar recalls the vow for intellectual liberation which ended *Iphigenia and Orestes*. When the United States enters World War I, he reflects, "Some day I'll go into the past and discover out of what we have come" (230). After he marries Neloa, he tells her: "Like most people you will believe nothing that shocks you. As for me I've taken to heart what Huxley wrote to Kingsley: Follow humbly, and to whatever abyss Nature leads, or you shall learn nothing. I have taken to heart what a high school teacher told me, one morning when I was out of my mind: Read the greatest books and follow them. Until we learn to accept the truths that outrage us, we may as well stand in the barn stanchions with the cows and bulls" *(Orphans,* 373).

By the time we reach the *No Villain Need Be* material, Vridar is not just primarily concerned with writing but is writing the kind of books which depend on researches into the past. His Washington Park experiences in Chicago had made him want to write about Christianity as a historical phenomenon (482), and, after Neloa's death, he seeks to find the artistic approach which will make possible the kind of excursion that his whole life had led him to want to undertake:

> He sensed his ageless heritage; now and then intimations came out of it and were hauntingly familiar, yet strange. Now and then he seemed in dreams to wander deep in it, to go far back, to lose himself in the primeval, where only his muscular self had meaning and use; where his only hungers were the eternal hungers—food and female; and his deepest emotions were fear and terror. Sometimes when awake he tried to project himself back into the black night of it; to imagine himself sitting in idolatrous worship by a fire, reading in its flame the soul of the world around him *(Orphans,* 609).

At the end of *No Villain Need Be* Vridar had made his analysis of himself and other people in terms of the auto-corrective theory. Fisher, as we have seen, had a kind of auto-corrective period; but in *Orphans* he drops these explanations entirely, a fact which changes radically the final book of the tetralogy. Vridar still has a split personality, but it is a split which stays with him. In *Orphans* Vridar is not the assured practicing amateur psychologist who leads others to health via the auto-corrective explanations, and many of the "preachments" of *No Villain Need Be* disappear. In *Orphans* Vridar dreams in symbols his whole life through; and, though he continues to analyze them, he does not attempt to have literal dreams as he did in *No Villain Need Be.* Nor does he urge the use of alcohol as a means to self-discovery. He also views sex differently; it is no longer a major means to the integrated personality. Thematically important to *No Villain Need Be* was Vridar's summer in Salt Lake City. There Vridar was supposedly getting sex out of his system and learning not to be ashamed of his body. A comparison of the two chapters concerning the Salt Lake City summer illustrates the effect of the removal of the auto-corrective theory.

In *No Villain Need Be,* Vridar's primary purpose in going West is to see if he is still "erotically evasive." There he has several sexual affairs, affairs which, we are told, are liberating. When he returns he tells Athene: "Mertyl, I think, is right again. Make the sex-obsessed person *think* sex, *act* sex, until he breaks that morbid fixation on it" (241). Vridar has apparently broken that fixation. Symbolically, he marries Athene, who has been, heretofore, his mistress. In *Orphans* Vridar is already married to Athene when he leaves: "Now she did not ask if he would see women. When he called himself babilan, she had known that he would. He wanted to shake off the curse that hung over him, but he was not going west primarily to see women who might welcome him there. He had to see his sons and parents. He wanted to see the mountains again, the rivers, the sagebrush plains to discover if he was now idealizing them, or if his greatest strength lay there" (621).

Fisher does not, however, treat Vridar's primary purposes in going west, but only that of seeing women, and he relates a new series of sexual affairs which are meaningless to Vridar and to the reader. The style of the revised version reflects the wasteland of the summer: "He and Carl went first to Salt Lake City, and when Vridar found that one of his former students was happy to see him and eager to go to bed with him, he called another, and still another" *(Orphans,* 621). The affairs in *No Villain Need Be* led Vridar to discover that he was still seeking Neloa. In *Orphans* he learns that sexual affairs are not to be taken so lightly as he had thought, and he feels guilty.

Apparently Fisher had come to feel that the answers of the tetralogy were rather shallow. If there is validity in seeing the healthy life as a matter of a balance between racial and ego drives, Fisher came to feel that merely stating Western man's problem in these terms would not help much. In the *Testament* Fisher tries to create fictional worlds where racial and egoistic drives are opposed. *The Divine Passion* (1948) shows a society in which the sexual desires and fulfillments are a major part of the religious rites. Through sexual congress the people achieve their greatest moments of oneness. But this is very different from Vridar's use of sex. The *Testament* indicates that *realizing* the conflicting drives is meaningful, but that talk of them in psychological jargon is not the way to realization. How does one know if his ego or racial drives are too strong? More crucially, how can these be balanced? In *Orphans* sexual license is not the answer.

Interestingly, Vridar relives, after his return to Idaho, several of the adventures of Ogden Greb from *Forgive Us Our Virtues*, a novel that explained Ogden and others in terms of the auto-corrective theory. In *Orphans* the same events bewilder Vridar, and he realizes how little of human nature he understands. A visit with Danny McGivern—Art Spikeman of *Forgive Us Our Virtues*—makes his doubts about his writing all the more intense and Vridar is the more convinced that he must make a long journey into the past.

Vridar's plans for a new novel of his life are interrupted by pressures for money, adding the important God or Caesar theme which goes hand in hand with the search into the past: what happens to the writer who has devoted his life to books for humanity and deepest truths rather than to books which make their appeal to the present market? Vridar has to set novel-writing aside and return to Montana College; later he accepts the position as Idaho director of the Writers' Project of the Works Project Administration. His experiences make Vridar think even more about the need for a deeper analysis of human nature, and these reflections in *Orphans* enable Fisher to use the Communism theme of the tetralogy in a more vital way and also to reinforce the thesis of the *Testament of Man*. Except for these adventures, the rest of *Orphans* is the story of Vridar's explorations into the race's past, explaining the man Vridar Hunter through them, and the difficulties he had getting published the truths he discovered.

Orphans in Gethsemane is a novel which covers the hero's experiences down a long path and to some dead ends. The novel time covers over half a century, and the ideas play over vast spaces of time. Whereas the tetralogy was tightened and defined by a more limited scope, *Orphans* is a much more panoramic affair, as a part of its subtitle suggests: *The Orphan and His World*. The panorama ends in long passages of talk which give new answers to the problems of the tetralogy.

III   A *World of Orphans*

The thesis which emerges from Fisher's new look at Vridar is captured in the title: *Orphans in Gethsemane.* In an interview with Alan Swallow at the completion of the *Testament,* Fisher summarized his novel's meaning:

> After projecting himself into many situations and sets of values, and making a long study of the lower animals, the protagonist is forced to conclude that few persons are adult. He sees a world of children. The reasons why children don't mature and become adult, *as the children of all other animals do,* he finds in the religious systems which are essentially an idealization of the family relationship. He suspects that "togetherness" in this country is being elevated to the status of a religion, because of fear.

To Swallow's request that he define *Orphans,* Fisher replied: "I think of the word more in a historical and philosophic perspective. Perhaps I can suggest it by saying that I see as the world's most unmistakable orphans that people who more than any other have praised the father (or Father), and more than any other have knelt in fear before the wailing wall."[3]

Dramatically, Fisher's theme finds its strongest expression in Vridar's relationships with his father and his brother. The earlier quotation about his father's castrating cattle indicates that the brutality of his father, Joe, first made Vridar ponder the nature of man. The treatment of Vridar's childhood in *Orphans* establishes clearly the son's hatred of his father. Instead of a father who was symbol of "all mighty and unafraid things" *(In Tragic Life,* 302), the Vridar of *Orphans* takes into manhood the memory of a father who was not only brutal but, Vridar later realizes, afraid. Since Vridar as a boy does not understand his father, his hatred keeps growing. This hatred is emphasized repeatedly in *Orphans* and becomes increasingly important in that part of the novel which covers Vridar's life beyond the time covered in the tetralogy. On his trip back to Idaho after he resigns his New York teaching position, Vridar reflects that a desire to understand Joe is one of his reasons for returning home.

In *No Villain Need Be,* Vridar thought he understood both father and mother. In *Orphans* he still understands his mother, but his father is a different matter. After he is settled in Idaho, Vridar goes ice fishing with Joe, and they almost drown in the swift and icy river; later father and son go down the treacherous river to Wyoming for logs and again come close to death. Vridar senses in both affairs that the father-son rivalry from childhood is still strong. Joe's unnecessarily cruel castrating, dehorning, and branding of the bulls seemed a threat to Vridar and his own masculinity. He discovers that as a man he still fears the loss.

The initiation of his exploration for the writing of his *Testament of Man* leads him to see a major link between his own life and early man's. He makes a note on one of his own problems, drinking: "I understand at last that as a child I felt horribly weak and inadequate and afraid around my father; getting drunk has been to some (possibly to a large) extent a compulsive wish to assert myself as an individual, to establish myself as a non-contemptible thing" *(Orphans,* 809).

Vridar's discovery that early man was often outraged and became schizoid because his vanity resented his inferior role in procreation gives him new insights on his father. Joe, too, was obsessed by feelings of insecurity, and fear became his master and made him a brute. Later Vridar researches the Judaic and Christian religions. What he discovers from that study shows him what he thinks is the final explanation of his insane youth: "Horrible fear of father and Father had driven him to a lunacy of prayer and tears and pleading" *(Orphans,* 877). Vridar, the son, had capitulated to the father, just as Joe, who to a much greater extent in *Orphans* is nurtured on the Bible, capitulated to the Father. The result for both was nightmare. Vridar's explorations reveal that sons in the Western world have consistently been capitulating to the fathers, and this accounts for the modern world's being, as Vridar puts it, a world of children and the twentieth century an Age of Violence.

Communism, one of the major causes of the present violence, is not in *Orphans* just one of the *isms* which the hero inspects in his efforts to find a workable code of life. It is, rather, an important illustration of the novel's thesis, a part of the father-son problem. In *Orphans* Vridar is a stronger advocate of socialism than in the tetralogy, and he earlier and more consciously realizes that socialism is a fraud. Thus it is that the Vridar of *Orphans* is not disposed to communism as Vridar of the tetralogy and those all about him are. In the tetralogy Vridar's case rested on the assumption that the world was not yet ready for communism and that the Communists did not have a satisfactory program worked out.

By the time of *Orphans,* of course, Vridar's fears of the tetralogy had been proven all too true. The leadership in the Soviet Union was no better than that of Nazi Germany and held human life as cheaply. Vridar in *Orphans* laments the tragedies of Poland and Hungary; after World War II, he and Angele visit Austria and mourn what the Communists have made of once happy Vienna. In *No Villain Need Be,* democracy is a romantic concept; in *Orphans* communism may be, Vridar says, "Man's most romantic notion so far" (638). In *No Villain Need Be* Vridar had stressed that the Communists did not have a workable program, but in *Orphans* he defends democracy and feels that it has not had a fair chance. His scorn of socialism and communism becomes complete after he has been working as director of the Idaho Writers' Project and has seen the inefficiency and waste of the New Deal. After studying American intellectuals who worship Franklin D. Roosevelt and those who advocate Communism, Vridar decides that they are children seeking a father. Having lost faith in God, they look for a substitute in Roosevelt or in Stalin and surrender their will to them. Those who turned to Stalin found a Joe quite like Vridar's father—obsessed by insecurity and frighteningly brutal. In *A Goat for Azazel* Fisher points out that emperors were finally made divine by those they had enslaved. In *Orphans* Vridar reflects: "Capitalism had been a pretty safe institution for the simple reason that no one had been able to make it divine" (755). After his observations of New Deal bureaucracy, he fears the undermining of the two-party system in the United States, and he resolves to give a part of his energy to its preservation; for children will capitulate to the father, and the fathers are usually like Joe Hunter and Joe Stalin.

Vridar's relationship with his brother also illustrates the father-son rivalry which Fisher sees as crucial to an understanding of modern man. In *No Villain Need Be* Vridar, with X and Y fairly well integrated, felt that he and his brother were now walking the same path (276). At the same point in *Orphans* Vridar senses no great fellowship with his brother—now named

Marion, rather than Mertyl—but Vridar craves such fellowship. A major part of the novel's final two books is concerned with Vridar's attempt to understand his relationship with his brother. Marion dies, Vridar knows, hating him; and Vridar's grief over Marion's death, combined with his disappointment in not finding a publisher for the later books of his great project, almost leads him to insanity. The puzzlement over Marion, never an important motif in the tetralogy, has been played upon throughout *Orphans,* and the estrangement for life clearly established (255).

The final paragraph of Part II of *Orphans* by its position, as well as its meaning, underscores the doubts about his brother which Vridar feels and it anticipates future doubts. *Passions Spin the Plot* ends with Vridar's calling Neloa to him and fearing their future together, and there is no mention of his brother. The *Orphans* section ends: "They went back to the house. Prudence came out to say she needed water. Then Marion came out with a pail and went to Neloa and put an arm around her; and together, with his arm around her, they walked down to the spring, a hundred yards away. Deeply troubled, Vridar stood in the yard and looked at them, and suddenly turned to see something strange in his mother's eyes" (370).

This passage not only foreshadows Marion's almost certain adultery with Neloa and the fathering of Neloa's second child, but raises the question of why Marion is as he is. The tetralogy was centered around Vridar and Neloa; in *Orphans* Vridar has to learn to understand not only Neloa but, and as importantly, also his brother. After Marion's death and after Vridar has made his search into the past, he realizes that the Vridar-Marion relationship is just the reverse of the Joe-Vridar relationship. To please his parents, young Vridar had tried to take care of Marion, to protect him from all dangers. He realizes that he has continued the habit throughout life. He has always tried to make Marion a success, to "push" him, much as the Vridar of the tetralogy pushes his brother's auto-corrective theory. Marion's death symbolizes his deep hate and revulsion for these parental pressures from Vridar. Vridar foolishly tells his brother who is near death after a severe heart attack that together they will still write the book on marriage. Marion violently sits up and, sickened by his life, knocks the tubes from his nostrils. The reader, of course, must accept Vridar's analysis. The entire story is given from his point of view, and Marion's consciousness is never displayed, but his hatred of and yet also a kind of reliance on Vridar is apparent.

Vridar and Marion follow each other almost uncannily. Vridar goes to Chicago, and Marion follows. After Neloa's death, Vridar goes to Baltimore because Marion is there, though also because he could not go west after Neloa's suicide and he cannot stay in Chicago. When Vridar leaves Wasatch College, he goes to New York City where Marion is practicing psychology. Vridar returns to Idaho, and Marion follows, as if to symbolize the tragedy of his own split personality—which has made of him a kind of Jim Jones and Harrison Hawke, the brilliant psychologist and the fraudulent, neurotic psychologist of *Forgive Us Our Virtues*. Vridar's parental care has made Marion a tragic orphan, or so Vridar feels. Chastened by his study of the past and what it has taught him about the present, in the final chapter of the novel Vridar asks Angele:

> Did I ever tell you of the time I carried Danny McGivern out of the whorehouse and almost dropped him when I saw his flabby drunken Irish face smiling up at me—for here is your child and he wants love. It was Danny who said that the world is full of Marions, every God damned one of whom hates the Vridars. The Marions want to be able to care for themselves, and the Vridars want to take care of them. There is a drive in every growing thing to become adult, but fear has made the older or more aggressive persons take tyrannical custody of the weaker. The heart of the Judean-Christian system is in the Vridar-Marion relationship (*Orphans*, 982).

The Judaic-Christian system has placed the Western world in a "darkness at noon." Vridar does not deny that the Western system once served Western man, but he feels that the time of that service has ended. The best scholarship has revealed that the bases for the system are untrustworthy. God is no longer in his heaven and all is not right in his world. Western man, however, has become accustomed to this dependence; so he looks for father substitutes. Hence, Fisher's title: the Father is gone; the Judaic-Christian religion has denied to man a Mother; so in the fullest sense of the word, modern man is an orphan. He is in his Gethsemane, a place of loneliness and sorrow trying to serve a Father—perhaps in a moribund church, perhaps in communism, perhaps in a family tragedy such as Marion's service to Vridar. Fisher's new message is hopeful, however. Noon means that half of the day is ahead. An awareness of his heritage can lead man to a yet firmer affirmation that no villain need be. Fisher's whole thesis is that intelligence has not been used as the standard for the Western world; when it is, the race will be on its way to becoming adult.

IV   *The Orphan as Writer*

The theme of Fisher's panoramic novel, then, finds its most dramatic representation in the new accounting of Vridar's relationships with his father and his brother, but these are interwoven with the theme in *God or Caesar?* which is also related to the *Testament* theme. The Western world, sickened and shackled by a family system which prevents most of its children from becoming adults, is not, of course, eager to accept Vridar's books, a new testament designed to liberate it. Most authors, Vridar discovers, are frightened children and have not, as he has, come to at least some notion of what adulthood is. They have their posturings and cults. Fisher displays the cult of the artist by sending Vridar on a trip with two friends to the D. H. Lawrence ranch where Frieda is exclaiming, "Veesiters! . . . Always veesiters!" (786). Visiting at the same time is Angus Boden, a thin disguise for W. H. Auden. The reader cannot miss the Auden identification because Vridar thinks he can write much better verse when asleep than those an editor had offered as evidence of Boden's brilliance. The lines are from Auden's Phi Beta Kappa poem:

> Thou shalt not do as the dean pleases,
> Thou shalt not write thy doctor's thesis
>   On education,
> Thou shalt not worship projects nor
> Shalt thou or thine bow down before
>   Administration.   (*Orphans,* 787)

Fisher also used Auden as an example of the orphan artist in *God or Caesar?* In fact, *Orphans* includes much of the material from Fisher's handbook for beginning writers of fiction. *Orphans*

propounds the same doctrines; the new slant is that it shows
Vridar learning the lessons at writers' conferences and in talks
with book reviewers, publishers, and a ghost writer. Most of the
lessons are painful. Vridar is repeatedly crushed by unfair
reviews, but Fisher believes the young writer should expect this.
He warns that, in a world of orphans, reviewers have their own
problems of insecurity; and, like the masses, most of them prefer
the tiger to the truth. Writers for Caesar will probably find a
market if they have talent, but, Fisher says, they will be exploiting
the weak. They can flatter reviewers and readers. They can
flatter and praise one another. They can endorse ale and
fountain pens.

The Vridar of *Orphans* has early dedicated himself to making
truth prevail and is, of course, unable to follow Caesar's code.
His ideal is the adult novelist, the one who has looked deeply
into his nature. When Vridar first wants to write he has little
idea why he wants to do so. Fisher, in his preface to *God or
Caesar?*, says that he wrote the book to tell the young writer
things he had not known and wished he had. One of the things
he explains is what kind of person the writer usually is: "The
artist is a kind of hybrid, half-man and half-woman, half-woman
and half-man."[4] In *Orphans* Vridar and Angele study the faces
of the poets on the cover of Oscar Williams' *Treasury of Modern
Poetry* to search for an adult. They find none. When Angele
sees Oscar Williams, she exclaims that he looks like a woman.
Vridar replies: "He's at least half-woman.... They all are, including the women" (902).

Fisher does not mean that the artist is a homosexual, but
that, because of his heritage and childhood, the artist has, on
one hand, a highly sensitive nature which makes him sympathize
and desire to "mother" and, on the other hand, a strong egoism
that makes him want to alter his environment. Because of this
duality, the artist is "neurotic, confused, frustrated, and rebellious."[5] The nightmare of Vridar's childhood made the split in
him so intense that he was often near insanity. His rivalry with
his father and his castration fears show how strongly he senses
his powerful feminine nature. He must fight to assert his
masculinity. Fisher finds the same need to assert masculinity in
a blood-and-guts writer like Hemingway.[6]

By proper balancing of the male and female, the artist finds in his art therapeutic treatment for his neurosis. If the writer realizes his potential, he will have satisfied the female because the writer feels himself "into another person's situation and *realizes* it not with one's own complex of ideas, prejudices, and beliefs, but with his."[7] And he will have satisfied the male, for the artist has created his own world, thereby altering his environment.

The artist worthy the name has dedicated himself to the race, not to his time. This is what Fisher means by being for God and not for Caesar. In *Orphans* Vridar makes this dedication early in life. His reading of fiction, though less central than in the tetralogy, also makes him condemn the false picture of life presented by a Willa Cather. Vridar, like Fisher in *God or Caesar?*, thinks that fiction should take as its basis a frank confrontation of human nature. The words of a character in a novel by Peacock can stand for the faith of each: "I conceive that men are virtuous in proportion as they are enlightened; and that, as every generation increases in knowledge, it also increases in virtue."[8]

Fisher defines his code of Realism in *God or Caesar?* by extended references to James Branch Cabell, a writer Vridar extols in the tetralogy. Cabell does to Vridar there what Fisher hopes his novels will do: show people the truth about themselves. The Cabell references are greatly reduced in *Orphans,* but not because Fisher has changed his mind about Cabell. The *Testament* is well under way by the time of *God or Caesar?* (1953) and Cabell is still praised in *Orphans.* Fisher's whole aim in the *Testament* is itself proof that he still values Cabell's direction. Fisher calls him the greatest Realist ever to write in America. In *God or Caesar?* he recommends to the aspiring writer *Beyond Life,* a book that makes a decided impression on Vridar in the tetralogy. *Beyond Life* is supposedly a defense of Romanticism, but everywhere Cabell is revealing the myths under the surfaces. Fisher declares: "the search for truth behind the appearances is still, in my opinion, the function of art."[9] Cabell is a great Realist because, although he defends "dynamic illusions," he is always showing them to be illusions. Most of what passes for Realistic fiction, Fisher says, is not. He terms *The Grapes of Wrath* "a romantic novel because it gives only the surface appearances" and is full of sentimentality. The deeper truths are not in the "surface materials" but in the myths behind them.[10]

However, Fisher and Vridar part company with Cabell and his defense of "dynamic illusions." In *A Goat for Azazel* a learned Jew's judgment echoes the message of the whole *Testament of Man:* "So we must ask if a myth is worth the horrors which it calls down upon those who believe it. . . . myth is a vehicle for truth. It may be a vehicle for error" (307). Fisher and Vridar attempt to give a greater affirmation to the future than to the dynamic illusion. Several times in *Orphans* and in *No Villain Need Be* Vridar sees the irony of Hamlet's famous eulogy of man: "What a piece of work is a man." Much closer to the truth, Fisher says, is Jurgen's judgment: "I am fettered by cowardice, I am enfeebled by disastrous memories; and I am maimed by old follies. Still, I seem to detect in myself something which is permanent and rather fine."[11] The greatest Realism would attempt to show that Jurgen has spoken truly of mankind, and this is the vision of *Orphans in Gethsemane*.

In *No Villain Need Be* Vridar, about to begin writing an autobiographical novel, took warning from Bob Clark, who was based upon Thomas Wolfe and who appears in only one chapter of the book. In *Orphans* he is renamed David Hawke, a thinner disguise for Wolfe; and he is given fuller treatment. His name is mentioned repeatedly thereafter. In *Orphans* Fisher also mentions Wolfe by name, and whether called Wolfe or Hawke, he becomes a symbol of the self-pitying, father-seeking orphans of American fiction. Fisher uses Wolfe in much the same manner in *God or Caesar?*, and he repeatedly illustrates his points with reference to him. The Wolfe references in *Orphans*, furthermore, relate to the *Testament of Man* scheme. Wolfe tried to explain Eugene Gant by looking at his boyhood; his efforts serve to remind Vridar that a better way is needed.

In *God or Caesar?* Wolfe is compared to Stendhal, a writer who in his lifetime never received anything comparable to Wolfe's acclaim, popularity, or financial success. *Orphans* sets up the same opposition. Vridar, from earliest years, has been something of a hero worshiper. With Athene he had seen himself as a Shelley during a stage in his "adolescence." The hero who serves as an increasingly bright beacon for Vridar is Stendhal because, like Vridar, Stendhal probed his own mind continuously, and he

honestly faced what he found there. Stendhal's writings anticipated future discoveries and gave light to great minds like
Freud. Vridar's aim in the *Testament of Man* is also to anticipate
the future by writing novels of the Vridars, the Eugene Gants
which will more fully explain why they are as they are:

> Stendhal, with the detachment of the scientist, had tried to
> understand himself. Nobody who called himself a literary critic
> had taken him seriously. Chateaubriand, that monumental ass,
> had been, in the opinion of the critics, writing one deathless
> masterpiece after another. Of him Stendhal had said, "What
> would be blasphemy to say of M. Chateaubriand now will be a
> truism in 1880." How true! Stendhal, knowing he was ahead of
> his time, or at least ahead of the critics, had addressed himself
> to posterity, predicting that he would be read in 1900. It had
> taken an ignorant mankind a little longer than that to discover
> him. My job, Vridar told himself, is to keep ahead of Stendhal,
> if I can . . . (*Orphans,* 673).

But, like Stendhal, Vridar found his efforts acknowledged by
only a few. One of Stendhal's novels sold only twenty-two copies,
and *The Red and the Black* never reached a second printing in
his lifetime. In *God or Caesar?* Fisher warns the young writer
that such neglect has been true of many of the giants: Lucian,
Juvenal, Keats, Meredith, Melville, Cabell. Vridar in *Orphans*
finds that the critics are unable to understand his works. He is
forsaken by those who promised to see him through and forgotten
by life-long friends. He gains almost nothing financially. But
he is faithful to the Stendhal ideal, and when the novel ends,
he feels that he has finished the course and fought the good
fight. He has fulfilled the vow he made at the end of the
Iphigenia and Orestes section. He has followed nature humbly
and, he feels, discovered some crucial things about where man
has been and why he is as he is.

V   *Broader Vision, Greater Art*

The *Orphans* version of Vridar's story surpasses the tetralogy
in important ways. With Fred T. Marsh, readers might easily
feel the tetralogy's answers to be too facile. Despite Fisher's
efforts to make Vridar an American symbol and to make the

telling of the story more than a mere Naturalistic report, the story sometimes approaches the "case history." But the hero of *Orphans* means a good deal more. Whereas Vridar in the tetralogy was often "anti-hero," Vridar in *Orphans* assumes significant stature as we view him against the background of myths which hold profound truths. Vridar is, in fact, a kind of Odysseus. He makes his mistakes, but Fisher is less determined to make his hero one with whom the reader will not identify. Fisher does not expect his readers to approve Vridar at every turn, but in the novel context one feels that ultimately Vridar, like Odysseus, is wiser than most of his kind.

The tonal difference in Fisher's new Vridar story makes an important artistic difference. The tetralogy has a textual unevenness essentially absent in *Orphans* because Fisher has more consistently treated Vridar as the hero of a more traditional narrative. In the tetralogy Fisher starts out like all Naturalistic writers; he seeks the causes which have made his hero as he is. The Naturalist seeks to understand, not to blame his characters. The older Vridar gets, the more Fisher tends to blame him. In *We Are Betrayed* Fisher is almost constantly lashing Vridar. Instead of the dispassionate Naturalist, the reader usually finds the condemning satirist, who by definition of satire, is judging his characters against moral standards. In *Orphans* the protagonist is often a satirist judging society, but he is more understanding than his predecessor in the tetralogy. More importantly, the novelist is not looking at his hero as the satirist does, but as the student seeking to explain. That Fisher has omitted all of the talk about his comic-book or funny protagonist indicates that he has recognized the inconsistent texture of his tetralogy. Tonally, the new Vridar has helped to unify the narrative as well as to insist on much larger dimensions to the story's meaning.

Vridar's characterization is not the only one which helps to make *Orphans* a work superior to the tetralogy. Of course, Fisher had a good deal in the way of vital characterization to start with, and in some cases he did not need to make many changes. The memorable portrait of Neloa is essentially the same as in the tetralogy. Vridar's second wife, Athene, however, is not more vividly portrayed; and Fisher's inability to give her interest in her own right, as he does Neloa, is a serious blemish in both

[66]

versions. Nevertheless, *Orphans* has a happier balance of characters than has the tetralogy.

In his discussion of "People" in *Aspects of the Novel*, E. M. Forster says that a proper balance of characters is the most crucial ingredient for a successful novel. Forster divides characters in novels into flat and round characters. "Flat" characters are one or two dimensional; that is, they are distinguished by one or two traits. Their value is that they are easily remembered and never need re-introducing. They give a sense of life because we know most people in this way. "Round" characters have depth; we know only a few people in this way. Forster says that the test of a round character is whether he is "able to surprise convincingly." A good novel will have a proper mixture of flat and round characters.[12]

One of Fisher's strengths as a novelist is his ability to create a great number of interesting characters, and the writer who treats a large number of years has to introduce many characters to keep the novel's sense of life vivid, for one keeps meeting new people. In panoramic novels (such as the tetralogy, considered as one work, and *Orphans*) the author needs to introduce new people as evidence of character development and of the passing of time. Thus, near the end of *The Old Wives' Tale* Arnold Bennett is still adding to his cast. We see less of Cyril as the years pass, but, even in lives so narrow as those of the old wives, new people come. Now we watch Lily Holl, Dick Povey, and Amy, the rebellious new servant, instead of the faithful Maggie or the ungrateful Cyril. It is, of course, all the more necessary that the novel about a hero with a great zest for life keep introducing new people. On the other hand, a novel with a more intensive (in contrast to the extensive or panoramic) structure is not likely to need new or many characters throughout. In *Howards End,* for example, Forster's cast is very small, and he does not need to keep introducing new people.

Nevertheless, Forster's point about a proper mixture of characters is a good one and also applies to the panoramic novel. An improper mixture of characters accounts for some of the critical objection to the tetralogy, which, like *Orphans,* has a quite consistent point of view.

In Tragic Life is generally considered the best of the tetralogy. A balanced presentation of character is a major reason for that

novel's success. Prudence, Joe, Vridar, Mertyl, Diana all move
and have life. Across the river from them dwells Charlie Bridwell,
who lives a philosophy of life directly opposite to that of Joe
and Prudence. So Charlie is important to the novel's meaning
as well as a colorful character. Charlie appears in the action
several times, and Vridar with a shudder often remembers him
and his son Jed. Vridar's relatives, though simpler, are vivid
and weave in and out. The reader is not likely to forget Vridar's
coarse and sometimes unfeeling grandmother, Rose; the Swede,
Borg; or the sensuous Agnes. Nephi and his family live on the
Hunter farm for two summers, and we see Hankie in several
incidents. Then there is Neloa and Vridar's bright memory of
her and also of the golden-haired Helen. In the school bullies
and in Vridar's high school teachers we get, for the most part,
brief sketches and perhaps an incident, but that is enough. These
minor characters are real because they interact convincingly with
Vridar whom we know so well.

If one compares Eugene Gant's school days with those of
Vridar, one simply does not find the same sense of life because
Eugene is not interacting with others. He is observing others
frequently, but usually one sees the others or Eugene, not both.
If one compares Laura James with Vridar's first loves—Neloa
and Helen—one again finds that Fisher has been more successful
in creating character to interact with character. The people who
make *Look Homeward, Angel* are Eugene and his family, and
in the family scenes Wolfe shows his most convincing interaction
of character, though frequently the family members are cari-
catures rather than characters. In *Of Time and the River* Eugene
is more completely an observer. We hear and see Starwick and
others but not often in interplay with the protagonist. Fisher's
range in *In Tragic Life* is greater. He has been able to surround
his hero with a large number of persons who engage the reader
and at the same time interact convincingly with the hero and give
balance to the whole novel.

Some of these characters are present in the other novels of
the tetralogy, particularly in *Passions Spin the Plot,* and so they
add force to those novels. Some, like Rose and Dock, do not
change; but, as Forster's discussion of flat characters indicates,
such characters help a novel. Fisher adds increasingly to the
characterization of Mertyl and Diana, who is excellent in *Pas-*

sions Spin the Plot. He also does what the panoramic novelist must do—introduce new characters. In *Passions Spin the Plot* Fisher presents the colorful A. M. ("Forenoon") McClintock. Forenoon is not a complex character, but he is certainly vivid. He is an orphan who is out to make his way in the world by petty thievery and trickery. His chief delight is seducing virgins, and he keeps track of his exploits in a notebook; yet when the United States enters the World War, he wants to fight to defend womanhood. He is a roisterer, a braggart, and a coward, and seemingly an unsuitable roommate for Vridar. But that Vridar lives with him for two years is wonderfully telling. The irony is just one of many which Fisher plays with. (One recalls that in *In Tragic Life* Vridar's bravest dreamings were usually followed by a mean trick from Old Charlie or by a visit from the cruel Jed.) While Vridar lives with Forenoon, he is holding blindly to the naïve view of women that Forenoon is always refuting. Vridar tries to reform the whore whom McClintock charitably tries to share with him. Thus Vridar's disillusionment over Neloa's questionable virtue has even greater ironical force, and Vridar's bitterness is double edged.

Fisher's success with Forenoon gives great vitality to the creation of Vridar's first college years. Wolfe presents no one so interesting as Forenoon in his treatment of Eugene at Pulpit Hill—no one who interacts with him in quite the same telling way. One remembers the amusing incident over the Latin translation, the pathetic death of Bob Sterling, and other brief vignettes; but again Eugene is more an observer of life than a participant. Eugene also becomes acquainted with prostitutes; and, although friends take him to the prostitutes, that is all we know of the friends. Wolfe's George "Monk" Webber is almost exclusively an observer when he is at college in *The Web and the Rock.*

Unfortunately, the largely successful balance of characters of *In Tragic Life* and of *Passions Spin the Plot* is not maintained in *We Are Betrayed* and *No Villain Need Be.* This is not to say that Fisher does not continue to introduce interesting characters; he does, but he does increasingly less with them, and *No Villain Need Be* has little concern with any personality except Vridar's. *We Are Betrayed*, however, does present a number of characters who make us believe in them at that time and who help to create the betrayed world against which Vridar reacts: Sergeant Alonzo Strumm and Lieutenant Jacks, Vridar's officers while in the army; the prostitutes of Idaho Falls in the post-war waste; Blanche Olson, the frustrated school teacher at Midwestern; Dennis Altrock, Vridar's strange graduate student friend at Midwestern, who has an uncanny cataloging mind, brute strength, and absolutely no moral sense. Even though Altrock and these others are not so functional as Forenoon, they help sustain attention: one always understands Vridar's interest in them, and they help to elucidate his character.

In *No Villain Need Be,* however, Fisher introduces less interesting characters, though not necessarily fewer. The crucial difference is that Vridar has become essentially a satirist, and his satiric verses, letters, and comments are the real substance of the novel. Vridar and Athene are almost the only characters significantly present. Vridar is an observer at the parties he attends just as George Webber is an observer at Esther Jack's party in *You Can't Go Home Again.* But, because Wolfe creates one scene with care and gives it symbolic meaning, his commentary on the same phase of American society is more forceful.

Fisher may have sensed the less happy balance of characters as the tetralogy progressed. In *Orphans* he tries to strengthen the part of characters who should have been important in the tetralogy but were not. But generally the characterizations of the tetralogy stand, and the section of *Orphans* corresponding to *No Villain Need Be* presents much less interesting characterizations than those in the material which preceded it. Fisher gives the reader many brief sketches, but he does not show his main characters interacting enough with people who, in the world of the novel, matter very much.

Although the tetralogy ends with a weak mixture of characters, *Orphans* is considerably better after this section because Fisher introduces many new characters who give a more vivid sense of life, and he continues to give a convincing illusion of life's being lived and of time's passing. He again has characters weaving in and out—characters who appear and reappear. Since Vridar has returned to Idaho, his parents re-enter the novel. They are, of course, much older, and their presence helps to increase a sense of time as well as to underscore meaning. Fisher also includes Danny and Gen McGivern, memorable as any of

Dickens' minor characters (unlike Wilma Regan, a former student who followed Vridar to New York and who is hostess at one of the "sophisticated" parties in *No Villain Need Be*). Although the McGiverns are borrowed from *Forgive Us Our Virtues*, they are more effective in *Orphans* because they are associating with Vridar rather than the relatively calm Ogden Greb.

The reader also meets Vridar's publisher Reuben Rhode, who appears several times. When Robert Bingham, the associate national director of the Federal Writers' Project, comes from Washington to try to stall the work of the Idaho Writers' Project, his visit makes good comedy not only because the fiasco over pictures for the *Guide* and the chase to the train occurred, but also because New Deal-hating Rhode is looking on. We have some idea of what Rhode is, and this scene at Rhode's house builds on Vridar's friendship with him, which makes more meaningful later his refusal to see Vridar through his historical series. Bingham, if not by name (although it may be suggestive), will probably be remembered after the reader has finished the novel.

Many of the persons Vridar meets working for the Federal Writers' Project are present for only a few moments, but most of them are genuinely interesting for the reader as well as for Vridar. Wilford Pogue, for example, is the spy Bingham puts on Vridar's staff. The ever-smiling Pogue was dismissed from his high school teaching job because he tried to seduce his girl students; his wife divorced him because he was too ardent; moreover, "He said he had read all of Freud and Jung and was ambitious to write a great work of philosophy. Plato was his favorite. Plato had said that the universe had its origin in time: if that idea could be integrated with Einstein's simple formula, man would have the key to the riddle" (*Orphans*, 749). Because of these intriguing characters, Fisher's readers see not only Vridar's difficulties on the Federal Writers' Project but also Vridar's reason for becoming increasingly dissatisfied with Socialism and Communism.

Fisher also introduces a large number of characters who, unlike the McGiverns, Pogue, and Rhode, only appear once in the novel. Some, like Bingham, are quite important for illustrating a central point. However, many of these characters, presented to illustrate that Vridar's is a world of orphans, could be omitted. Even though the reader may feel the number of such characters excessive, he will doubtless be struck by Fisher's talent at creating arresting characters.

Fisher usually introduces these characters with a sketch. But whereas *No Villain Need Be* presented essentially only the sketches, *Orphans* surrounds them with more developed scenes, with characters who reappear. The hero is so busily and convincingly engaged in either the Writers' Project or his vast historical series (compare with the frenzied work on a doctoral dissertation and teaching experiences in *No Villain Need Be)* that he lends life to the persons around him, for he is always a participator. Wolfe in *You Can't Go Home Again* also relies heavily on the character-sketch technique. He introduces a character, gives him his scene. But usually the protagonist, George Webber, is only observing the minor character; consequently, the novel is indeed segmented. *Orphans,* however, is a continuous flow of experience, and it gives a sense of that flow because of an essentially successful creation of minor characters who interact with the hero. And because *Orphans* gives a heightened sense of that flow, it is a significant improvement over the tetralogy.

Stylistically, *Orphans* is frequently more polished, more precise, though by no means does Fisher without exception heighten the illusion of reality behind every change.[13] But ultimately *Orphans* is the greater book. Fisher is more consistently a Naturalist, and one who looks to the myths. He wisely abandoned his attempt for a comic novel. As a functional unit of the *Testament,* *Orphans* may be labeled tragi-comedy. Vridar—and Western man—has been repeating age-old patterns, sometimes comic, sometimes tragic, as his myths victimize him. Whereas the tetralogy is perhaps most poignantly the story of a terribly morbid young man's search for health, *Orphans* is the fulfillment of a promise to explore the race's past as fully as possible—to journey into Meredith's Woods of Westermain. This novel is a brave and worthy addition to American letters.

CHAPTER 4

Journey to the Past:
The Testament of Man

O NE of the most monumental fictional projects ever under-
taken in America is Vardis Fisher's *Testament of Man:
Darkness and the Deep* (1943); *The Golden Rooms* (1944);
Intimations of Eve (1946); *Adam and the Serpent* (1947); *The
Divine Passion* (1948); *The Valley of Vision* (1951); *The Island
of the Innocent* (1952); *Jesus Came Again* (1956); *A Goat for
Azazel* (1956); *Peace Like a River* (1957); *My Holy Satan*
(1958); and *Orphans in Gethsemane* (1960). That this series,
Fisher's labor of love, met for a time with almost complete
neglect is almost surprising—given the general positive response
the first volumes received. While none of them received the press
or sales of the Harper Prize Novel *Children of God*, both *Darkness and the Deep* and *The Golden Rooms* have more intensity
and beauty than the Mormon novel. The point that reviewers—
including Diana Trilling, Clifton Fadiman, and Fred T. Marsh—
made about those books is that they are exciting reading. Not all
of the novels that followed them have the same power; but, like
the first two volumes, they have deserved more attention than
they have received.

The project is, of course, frighteningly ambitious. Fisher aimed
at presenting as imaginative experience the evolution of man's
"soul" from its first stirrings to the present day—so far as modern
scholarship would enable him to trace human strivings and
hungers. He realized the immensity of the project, but he
thought of his novels as pioneering in a fruitful direction. The
novels, Fisher hoped, would help the general reading public
to be aware of the causes of its painful heritage, a heritage
which Fisher's experience would not let him deny. The autobiographical Vridar comes to feel the frustration of this evangel-
ical hope: the people willing to follow through on such ad-

ventures are generally not the people who read novels! But
Fisher comforted himself with Cabell's dynamic illusion—that
he was writing for future generations more than for the present
one. If Fisher were writing for present fame, he could have
taken ample warning from Cabell's experience that the general
public soon tires of a long series.

I Prehistoric Man

Fisher has frequently been called a propagandist, and the
Testament, to be frank, is didactic. Fisher has a message, and
he does not wish anyone to misunderstand him. He regrets the
modern prejudice against authorial intrusions, which he considers to be the cream of many of the great Victorian novels.[1]
Some readers will be greatly annoyed at the didactic in Fisher.
Anyone reading the *Testament* straight through may be irritated
by repetitions; though some are unnecessary within a work,
Fisher rightly repeats the central themes of a previous novel.

However, particularly in the first two volumes, *Darkness and
the Deep* and *The Golden Rooms,* one is impressed with the
way Fisher has surmounted the didactic dangers. The novels
are, if anything, sympathetically imagined as experience. While
few people have taken the trouble to imagine earliest man,
Fisher's characters are vividly there and in action. To write
convincingly about early man presents a more than ordinary
challenge as the few writers who have tried their hand at it
show. H. G. Wells was willing to go backward in space and
time as well as forward, but his *A Story of the Stone Age* (1897)
is more entertaining than suggestive of the period. Jack London
wrote about the tree people in *Before Adam* (1906)but in the
worst possible point of view for a story of primitive man—first
person—which London tried to make believable by having a
modern man dream back into the race memory. Mary Johnston's
The Wanderers (1917) was more successful though depending
on a tableau effect rather than a vividly imagined era. Johannes
Jensen's *Fire and Ice* (1923) suggested more clearly what the
appeal of earliest times might be in fiction.

Fisher's books borrowed nothing from these earliest efforts
to picture primitive man, and setting his books next to them
emphasizes how much more powerfully the experiences of

Fisher's characters are imagined. The research behind his books is tremendous, but Fisher has realized with considerable success what the researches show life to have been. Generally, but not exclusively, his method is to imagine what Vridar would have done in the times Fisher considers.

Before presenting the story of the first primitive Vridar, Fisher opens *Darkness and the Deep* in a beautifully rendered backdrop, which gives not only an account of the creation of the earth and of how it evolved to become able to sustain human life, but also a forceful statement of Fisher's belief in human intelligence and the value of a long look at the race's progress. He emphasizes that there was a great deal of waste in nature's vast laboratory and that she had a sardonic humor in her creation of grotesques. The killers made the greatest advancements and came to have dominion over the earth. One of the killers, man, also became a creature of hope. Vardis Fisher's hope for man refuses to die, and he trusts something more precious than the world has seen will emerge from man's perilous journey:

> The insatiable hunger of human striving would have it so. The price we have paid for a little beauty and a little good will would have it so. The long pilgrimage out of darkness towards light, out of slime towards cathedrals of the soul, declares not only that nothing is lost but that something is gained from each cycle of sensate things through birth and age and sleep. Being what we are by no will of our own, by no wisdom or no ignorance that is ours, in that feeble hope we must find our meaning and our destiny, or there must be only folly and futility of creatures driven by universal laws to seek, and denied by those laws the eventual goal.
>
> If we are only the blind driven down to the seas, it would be a senseless pain to look back upon the dark and bloody trail which we have followed. If beyond our perishing in our present form, when our earth shall have finished its cycle, and shall have had its cold stone drawn back to the incandescent womb— if, then, all that was best in us shall become part of another world in another time, using not the pettiness of our personality but the stuff of our dreams, we can believe that nothing we have suffered has been in vain. If this is so, then a look backward becomes an adventure in self-discovery which the intelligence of man owes to his spirit, and the dark and brutal past becomes a searchlight that we can turn upon the future (7-8).

Against the terror and the poetry of the world's becoming, Fisher tells the story of one of earth's first geniuses—Wuh, who discovered the use of the club. In Wuh and his first woman, Murah, one finds the promise of the race.

Wuh's people have not learned to use fire and know it only as a thing to fear; they have not learned to use shelters; they are barely down from the trees and wander for their food. Moreover, they are quite unaware of being different from other animals. They have, of course, little language; only the brightest of them are just learning to make the simplest words. They have no names, really, but Fisher supplies sounds a chimpanzee might make for the sake of telling Wuh's story. It is not a long one, but it is richly suggestive of all the Vridars who are to follow. Fisher evokes a strong sense of the groping for thought in the simple minds of his people. The plot has a journey motif though the travelers have little sense of going anywhere. When the story ends, however, Wuh has arrived somewhere. The faint yearnings of conscience or soul, a desire for fellowship beyond the sexual embrace, have appeared.

The first part of Wuh's story is his adolescence, suggestive and amusing in its own right, though doubly so if we know Vridar's story. Wuh, like Vridar, is brighter than his peers, but he is a physical weakling and sexually frustrated. Because he is more intelligent, Wuh suffers more than Hwah, the strong young man who, like Wuh, is biding his time to take over the guardianship of the clan from Ho-wha. All of the males envy Ho-wah because as lord he alone can embrace the females of the group. Watching Wuh and the other frustrated males, we sense how the human race has evolved as a family unit and how deep fear and hatred of the father figure goes.

Denied sexual fulfillment and security, Wuh pushes his mind further than he might have. He craves the attention of the group, but gets very little of it. He tries to call attention to his importance by making the first movements toward art—dancing, music, body adornment. But he gets all too little attention to please his gnawing ego, and Ho-wah frequently reminds him where his place is—at the outer edge of the circle.

Like everyone else, Wuh is hardly conscious of time or another's welfare. After a python kills Kuoh, she is forgotten. When Ghoo, an ugly old woman, is too weak to travel one morning, the group abandons her with little fuss—and with her the ugly dwarf who remains with Ghoo because she has taken care of him for so long that he is dependent on her. The aged do not matter much; all of the race's efforts, most especially those of the mothers, is concentrated in the young.

Fisher renders these and other scenes with forceful economy. Though his characters meet danger and death constantly, Fisher is never melodramatic or sentimental.

At the end of Part I, Wuh finds his opportunity. One night the bold Hwah decides the time to fight Ho-wah has come. Wuh gets caught in the fight and, though unconscious of his innovation in the art of battle, slays Hwah with a huge stone, then seizes the young girl Murah, and dashes off into the forest to start his own clan.

Part II is the ironic story of a Wuh who has won the kingdom of women he has dreamed about in Part I. He, like the other men, had always wanted as many women as possible, but after he drives one lord away and kills another, thus increasing his group, he has complications he had not considered. Wuh is an amusing fellow as he tries to keep his family in order. And the sexual paradise he had craved is simply not his. When the women are pregnant or lactating, and that is much of the time, they scorn the male; and Wuh suffers grievously at this injustice of nature.

Thus frustrated, Wuh goes exploring. He discovers the use of the club and learns new power. The python becomes a little less awesome after Wuh kills one with his club and realizes some of the potential of the marvelous weapon in his hand. Later his mind expands in the male direction of power and dominion as he anticipates the biblical injuction: "Go to the ant, thou sluggard." Wuh watches the ants do battle as an organized army against a hornet's nest and has intimations of other regiments.

Fisher's emphasis, however, is not all on the male. The egoistic strivings of the Wuhs would not have taken the race very far. Wuh's woman Murah is every bit as remarkable as he. Wuh is a dreamer, an explorer; but Murah capitalizes on his inventions and sees the potential for the race, for her babies. She is practical. She, not Wuh, senses how his first random shelter could be useful. It was she who put a stop to the endless wanderings. She would move only with a reason. And she is the first to use language.

All in all, Fisher's characters in *Darkness and the Deep* are, though primitives, admirable and remarkably varied. Though the main characters are exceptional for their epoch, they are completely convincing. Their story is fast moving and, one feels, important. We have come a long way from the "darkness and the deep" in the powerful final chapter when Wuh finds the old man whose family he had stolen, hiding, frightened and alone, in an outcropping of stone. Huge flesh-eating birds fly above the old man and await his death. Wuh feels no pity, no mercy, no love for the frightened man whose end he reads in the old eyes. Nor is there an urge to kill. But Wuh recognizes the old man as one of his kind and perhaps wishes to protect him. He perhaps has intimations of his own death some day. Wuh rushes furiously at the birds. In this act of fellow involvement, Wuh's emotions are the most complicated he has yet experienced; and, as Wuh walks away to his family, he is not quite the same man.

Although there may not be as much humor in *The Golden Rooms* as in Wuh's story, again there is abundant variety, and it is one of the most tightly knit books Fisher has written. As sheer narrative it is much superior to the highly praised *Children of God*. Although it portrays both a Neanderthal and a Cro-Magnon society, the novel has a marked concentration, and the book is one rather than two.

Part I tells the story of the Neanderthal man Harg. Like Wuh, Harg is a frustrated Vridar. He is a solitary youth who craves admiration. He, too, dwells on the outer circle of his society until one day he discovers the use of fire. For Harg and his people the discovery is truly revolutionary. Into the dark terrors come the golden rooms, and Fisher dramatizes how fire brought light to human minds. It changes the whole pattern of life and incidentally makes Harg the tyrant of the group. Harg's people come to feel that he is a maker-of-magic, and he assumes a most hallowed position in the group. He is a stronger, more cunning protector than those who earlier relied on brute strength and, therefore, receives greater adulation.

Harg relishes his new position, but with his arrogance a sense of responsibility is kindled, especially after he observes how the male boar cares for his family. Exulting in new power, Harg becomes a fairly dynamic leader. In fact, he molds the community into a much more meaningful unit. For the first time in history people combine for a project of magnitude. Under Harg's direction they trap a woolly mammoth and make their kill with fire. The immensity of the occasion is greater than the simple people can grasp. Not only has the fire permitted the slaying of such a huge beast, but also it has provided new protection at night from their enemies and from cold. After Harg's people glut themselves for two weeks, the meat turns putrid, and they accidentally discover the value of cooking: the cooked meat does not make them ill. They also learn that the fat burns and soon grasp the first candles to give further illumination to the golden rooms.

The clever Harg also divines a further momentous use for fire: the capture and retention of caves for their dwelling. Consistent with the pattern he established in *Darkness and the Deep,* Fisher has Kayah, the most vital female of the family, see how magnificent Harg's idea really is, and it is she who pushes him to its implementation. The chapters describing the capture of the cave from the bears and the group's defense of it present a vivid and heroic action. The narration is not only good story; it stresses the increased value of the community effort. The fate of the individual is simply not important, and, though individuals perish in the securing of the cave homes, the victory is by no means Pyrrhic.

The advantage of the fire and the cave brings attendant disadvantage. The women have their purpose in children and experiment with clothing, but the fire makes Harg lazy. He is too prone to glory in past achievement and becomes increasingly tyrannical. None of the men is eager for winter hunting. Only severe necessity finally pushes them from their shelter, and one day the now arrogant Harg experiences new terror. Out hunting he discovers strange human tracks.

The tracks belong to Gode, whose people have long known the uses of fire which Harg has just discovered. Fisher juxtaposes against the accomplishments of Harg, the greatly advanced Cro-Magnon people; for nature's way has never been in a straight line. Harg's people are ugly compared to the tall, erect, handsome people of Gode. Remarkably advanced, the Cro-

Magnons have a language much more complicated than the rudiments of the Neanderthals. They have more carefully defined concepts of home; and, though they meet their neighbors occasionally for hunting parties, they have a heightened concept of the sanctity of each man's home. They are beginning to form taboos, and the men are learning the value of art for their lonely hours.

Gode is, in fact, a distinguished representation of Fisher's theory of the artist. From its beginning art has served as therapy to a frustrated ego. Women found meaning and extension of themselves in their children and were satisfied. Early man, however, felt completely unrelated to the process of birth. When he later learned his part, he felt it to be rather insignificant. The women usually had little use for men except as protectors and food getters. So the cave man Gode, more intelligent than most men of his time and more frustrated by the neglect of his importance, turns to art:

> He drew those animals he most admired and envied. As in drinking their blood and eating their hearts he thought he partook of their qualities, so in setting their likeness on stone he was trying to master and assimilate them. He was extending himself into the world and enveloping, by becoming intimate with them, the qualities he wished to have in great measure. He was altering his environment by bringing the beasts, obedient and subject to his will, into his home. In fancy he was enlarging his view, exploring his hidden powers, and identifying himself in a kind of fellowship with all the things he held in esteem (193).

Gode also tries to add to his importance through his association with a wolf cub which follows him after he has killed its mother. The women—especially the tyrannical Marrig, who anticipates the matriarchal society of the next two volumes of the *Testament* —want Gode to kill the "enemy." They cannot understand their man's refusal to do so. Gode cherishes the dog because he feels a need for greater fellowship than he has known. The dog becomes a friend and finally has infinite value because other men in the community envy Gode his great distinction, for none of them has ever had a dog. Gode's relationship with the dog is to be more important to the society than they could imagine. When the novel ends, Gode's life has been transformed.

Journey to the Past

People had seen only visible dangers heretofore, and happiness was, though not steady, much more obtainable than at the end of the novel when Gode experiences a frightening un-seen world. His dog is perhaps decisive in preparing him for the religious awakening he undergoes.

Unlike Harg, Gode is an excellent hunter and provider for his family. One day he organizes a horse stampede. The take is so great that he decides to move his family to the game area, which happens to be the section of land where Harg's people dwell. Gode and the other men who moved with him are amazed at the strange, ugly creatures they find. They will not admit their kinship to such monstrosities, and the first organized war follows —one fought, of course, for the loftiest principles. Wuh's lesson from the ants is realized. After a first day's kill, Gode is troubled upon close examination of the corpses: the dead somehow seem related to his people. On his way back to his family, something strange happens to Gode. He comes across a snake nest. The snakes are hidden in crevices. When partridges drop to drink, the snakes seize them:

> Gode stooped and peered before one of the chambers. Then he reached in with his lance and stabbed a serpent's head. The fangs relaxed, and Gode took the wounded bird in both hands and looked at it. He felt blood on one hand and when he turned the bird over he saw blood on the feathers. In any former evening of his life he would have snapped the head off the partridge and taken it home to eat; but there was a different emotion in him tonight. He set the bird down to see if it could stand, and at once it flew away. That pleased him. He marked its flight for a few moments and then stabbed another serpent, and a third and a fourth, releasing the birds that could fly and laying the others on the ledge at his feet. All but two of the birds flew away. These two were so badly wounded that they were dying; but Gode did not pull off their heads. When he turned homeward he carried them in his arms and from time to time he stopped and set them on the earth to learn if they could fly (270).

That night he dreams strange dreams, and when his dog is missing the next morning, he has the first notion of a ghost: a ghost of one of the dead men had stolen his dog. Gode no longer lives in one world, but two.

The climax of the war ensues with an attack on Harg's group—a group all the more disturbing and offensive to Cro-Magnon vanity because it also uses fire. The battle with Harg's family is more intense; but just as his victory is certain, Gode again does a strange thing: he saves one of the babies for restoration to his women, who recognize immediately that the creature is human and requires loving care. Once again Fisher emphasizes that women have stronger racial instincts.

But life can never be the same for Gode—he has undergone a profound change. The power of the dead is now a frightening reality, and Gode tries frantically to placate their ghosts. When the rainy season comes, storm is no longer merely natural; it is supernatural as well. *The Golden Rooms* ends with a memorable scene in which the transformed Gode, frightened with the new terrors of the unseen world, moans the first human prayer. When portraying such agonies of the human heart, Fisher is at his best.

II *The Matriarchal Society*

Intimations of Eve and *Adam and the Serpent,* volumes three and four of the *Testament,* portray life in a matriarchal society. *Testament* readers are prepared to believe in such a society because of convincing intimations in *Darkness and the Deep* and *The Golden Rooms.* The most wonderful thing in the lives of the fear-ridden creatures Fisher has shown is birth—and this miracle is the province of the female. Wuh, Harg, and Gode can really offer nothing in comparison. In the Cro-Magnon society of *The Golden Rooms* the grandmother is already assuming dictatorial powers, and special taboos around female functions have taken root.

But although the reader should be willing to grant Fisher his premises, he is likely to find the matriarchal novels less satisfying than the intriguing opening volumes, but perhaps the dissatisfaction may not be entirely Fisher's fault. He may wish us to feel the degradation that the religious forms he portrays cause his characters, and they are certainly people in bondage. A part of the excitement of the first two books is in the shared advancement of the race and the expansion of the human spirit. In *Intimations of Eve* Fisher shows some progress: the inventions of the chimney, the canoe, and, importantly, the domestication of herd animals. But no discovery parallels Wuh's mastery of the club, Harg's mastery of fire, or Gode's spiritual "awakening." The first two novels have a stark realism, but they have thematic grandeur as well. The geniuses of the matriarchal novels (who are again in the Vridar tradition) have less to recommend them. They are the first prophets, interested mainly in refining religious rites. They face fewer dangers from the outside world, but the dangers from the unseen world are more crucial. So they turn their attention to metaphysics.

The themes of the matriarchal novels have, of course, great significance for the Vridars that are to be, but they do not lend themselves so readily to the high adventure Fisher handles so well. The characters are pettier, and Fisher's comments about them and his asides about the modern world—in the absence of the magnificent themes of the first books—call more attention to themselves, and the repetitions are more obvious. The matriarchal novels have more characters and the action is less concentrated. As pure story, they are less memorable.

Intimations of Eve recounts the growing hatred between the grandmother of a "family" group and her genius son Raven. This rivalry is the dominant thread of the episodic narrative and one Fisher sustains nicely, but the Moon and the Mother are firmly established in the society, and Raven's life is one of frustration and desperation. Raven gropes toward a concept of sin which will free him from the bondage of a system based on the strictest division of labors and which leaves him, as a male, without much opportunity to feed his ego. More than a complete action—such as a progress, a journey—*Intimations of Eve* recounts a condition of life. Raven is a heightened example of the frustrated male in a female society; in his unconscious he gropes toward a notion of an Eve responsible for evil. He leads an unfulfilled sex life. Women will tolerate an embrace only occasionally; they are unaware that the male has any function in the birth process.

One realizes that Raven is subtly changing religious forms, but the facts of birth are now too much against him. The culminating blow to his increasing arrogance comes in a magnificent scene in which the grandmother saves the Moon Woman who is being destroyed by a monster (really an eclipse of the moon). Raven's time is not yet.

The memorable eclipse scene is but one of the several events that give variety to the pace of the narrative. Fisher has been able to imagine his primitive people in several situations and attitudes. There is even a good deal of humor in the rivalry between Raven and the matriarch. At the end of the novel Fisher has his little joke on the arrogant mothers. The grandmother discovers a family with a goat—a milkgiver. She sends Raven to steal the amazing creature. Raven steals the mother goat and a female baby. The grandmother, by introducing the domestication of animals and scorning to take the ram, unknowingly undermines her own special position in the community.

In *Adam and the Serpent* the matriarchal society is in its last stages. We have come a long distance from Raven's bondage, and in many ways life is a more complicated affair. The notion of marriage is much more clearly defined—though it is not a very blessed institution. Politics is a more serious game, and religious rites—in comparison to Raven's—have become greatly refined. In fact, the whole basis of the society is being questioned. Most of the *Testament* novels treat a time of stress and transition; in *Adam and the Serpent* Fisher is trying to suggest one of the most revolutionary changes in man's history: the change to a patriarchal society.

The "genius" of the decaying society is Dove, the scorned husband of the daughter of Rainmaker, the village queen. Usually the curses of one so powerful as Rainmaker would cause a man to die, but Dove mysteriously survives the curses and tries to develop his own magic. More than any other character in the book, Dove—who, because of the highly developed division of labors which gave the most important tasks to women, does not have much to do—ponders the phenomena of the natural world. He makes some amazing discoveries. His people have unknowingly been attracted to many phallic symbols—an important one being the serpent, which has a mysterious power of renewal. Dove sees in the penis—and hence the male—the same eternality that had been the province of the Moon and woman. Creation was not exclusively female! His heresies multiply. He sees the sun as an eternal father, thus giving more friendliness to his world, for the father watches while the mother sleeps.

Dove's people are ready for these more complex views. They have come to realize, probably from watching their domesticated animals, that the female must be impregnated. Birth is still more a spiritual than a biological thing with them, hence male *spirits* do the impregnating, though occasionally these spirits assume a human form. But Dove also notes with triumph that the males of the domesticated animals rule supreme, and he comes to find in women the source of all evil. The sin concept Raven groped for now becomes stated heresy. And, though Dove pays for his heresy with his life, his views have gained some hold and will certainly grow. Because of him a human for the first time is condemned for her "sin." The gathered crowd readily gives credence to Dove's accusations that the woman Passion has sapped the precious masculinity of the impotent Ram.

Fisher portrays the decline of the female society at several levels. For one thing, Rainmaker's position is not secure; she has a rival for chief magic-maker in the woman Firetaker. And Dove is not the only male causing trouble. Taboos are giving way everywhere. Owl comes to believe Dove and invades sacrosanct ground. Even the conventional Falcon defies a taboo by too early seeking his wife's bed. Rainmaker sees all about her signs of moral decay, and she strives desperately to preserve her waning prestige.

The novel's action is the story of her struggle and the use of magic and countermagic. The people of the village live in a kind of wasteland of matriarchal society. Readers may tire of the erotic shenanigans of the three suitors for Myrtle, Rainmaker's granddaughter, but Fisher means to show a decadent society. The intensification of the rivalries in the second half of *Adam and the Serpent* gives it more dramatic force than *Intimations of Eve*. And though the "resurrection" of Lotus near the end may be a bit forced, Fisher utilizes it skillfully to hasten an end to Rainmaker's rivals. On a dramatic level alone, however, Fisher has made clear that her victory is only a seeming one.

III   *The Hebraic World*

The Divine Passion carries the *Testament* to the dawn of recorded history and of Hebraic culture, a culture of vast significance for Fisher's series since it has so profoundly affected the course of the Western world. The novel also raises the level of the *Testament* as literary creation, for it is decidedly superior to the novels dealing with a matriarchal society. Vestiges of mother worship remain, but the priestess' power is only a shadow of that possessed by a Rainmaker. The father, the sun, is now worshiped as the vital force.

Knowing in particular *Adam and the Serpent* gives added force to *The Divine Passion*, for the later novel is in many ways an about-face of the events of the earlier book, but with a more concentrated story line. We again have the barter for a bride, but the priest rather than priestess officiates and father rather than mother profits. Again the established social order begins to crumble, this time under a much sterner and more complex code—one which pushes women to the degrading position Dove had wished for them. The struggle for love and power involves many characters very much like those of the earlier novel: Myrtle becomes Alzina; Falcon becomes Laurel; Basket becomes Beth; Ram becomes Yescha. Fisher clearly expects his readers to see the old problems and patterns but more complicated subterfuges.

Almost any one of the comparisons suggested above reveals the more artful treatment in *The Divine Passion*. Fisher delays Yescha's entrance into the novel, though he indicates earlier that he is a threat to the existing order. Yescha is the first prophet in the series who lives a religion—and he does so agonizingly. The importance of the neurotic prophet increases as his fortunes interact with those of the central character, Adom. His insane castration and death fittingly end the novel.

The Divine Passion presents, however, a striking departure from the pattern of the earlier *Testament* novels. The central character is not in the Vridar tradition. The superior intelligence is the priest, Rabi, who is a part-time skeptic but no reformer, and he plays in the wings of the action. In this novel Fisher takes as hero a Babbitt of the sun-worshiping society. Adom is a representative man, even though he is a patriarch with civic duties. Because Fisher focuses almost exclusively on Adom and his most intelligent wife, Narda—who is the deceitful Eve that her foolish man has made her—the story moves more definitely in a single direction than does *Adam and the Serpent* where point of view is too shifting.

Were the ending not so vivid in its intimation of so much pain for future generations, one would call *The Divine Passion* a comedy; for it is a comedy of married love and evasions in the cradle of civilization. Adom-Babbitt, so proud of his community position and physical fitness (he has parts like a god's), makes blunder after blunder without ever realizing what an amusing figure he is. He first tries to bed the beautiful Alzina; he pays a fantastic bride price for her, ostensibly for his son, but the wedding fruits go to the priest and the husband. Adom tries to enrich his coffers by demanding a return of the bridal price for his worthless wife Abra, who has returned to her father, but he purchases another wife instead, a beautiful one who scorns his advances. He fails to appreciate the healing female virtues of Beth. The cunning Narda succeeds in her efforts to have a liaison with Rabi whereas Adom never enjoys Alzina—as Narda had planned that he should not. Continually duped, Adom receives credulously the absurd report of his son about their weak and degenerate enemies (ancestors of the Hittites) and goes off to battle confident of victory. He loses his life in a rout. In his burial rites, complacent and wishful "Booster" Adom, gets the flattering epitaphs which are a final mockery to a man of property and position.

But Adom's defeat, also a kind of defeat for Rabi, is Yescha's victory. The prophet of doom undermines confidence in the sun worship, the worship of the life principle. The Hittites' defeat of Adom's troops give him the opportunity he needs, for the signs for victory had been propitious. Why had the gods, then, not cooperated? The prophet says a wicked priesthood is at fault, and he accuses Narda of sapping the life energy of the priest and offers himself in propitiation. Through his death, he thus gains the at-onement with his people which his physical deformity had prevented. The castrate has triumphed, but *The Divine Passion* scarcely leads to the conclusion that the new religion will be desirable, for Yescha has preached guilt and dogma rather than joy and vision.

Valley of Vision is a novel of King Solomon and his times. In portraying Israel's famous king, Fisher writes a novel in which the most convincing action is on the level of philosophical discussions; for more than any of the preceding novels, *Valley of Vision* is a novel of ideas, and the climax is a verbal duel between Solomon and the Yescha of the novel—Ahijah. It is also a departure from the pattern of the other novels because the hero is based on an actual person. Fisher admits that he has probably made Solomon a greater king than he was, but otherwise the novel is in accord with the best authorities available. Perhaps it is best to call Fisher's Solomon a symbol of light in a rather dark and forbidding Hebrew world. Solomon desires a large human fellowship, a religion of the valleys, and one that contains the tenderness of the mother which the Yeschas have undermined. In the readable set of notes at the end of the novel, Fisher points out that the Hebrews were a curious people for having a religion with only a male deity, for all of their neighbors worshiped a goddess. Though the Hebrews borrowed much from their neighbors' religions, they scorned the mother concept, and this Fisher thinks accounts for the Jewish isolation in the world. Solomon tells his Egyptian queen at the end of the novel: "my people will never mix with other people until they have a Mother" (400).

The peculiar isolation of the Jews in the Western world was really a conscious choice—*Valley of Vision* and the following *Testament* novel, *The Island of the Innocent,* declare, and both raise the question of how different modern history would be had the Jews taken the path of Solomon. Fisher challenges his readers to imagine other possibilities for humanity had other decisions been made at the times of special crises which *Valley of Vision* and *The Island of the Innocent* treat.

To make real the historical option in *Valley of Vision,* Fisher juxtaposes mainly two cultures—that of the desert, infant Hebrews and that of the established Egyptians. In two ways the novel utilizes the visiting foreigner motif. Early in the novel, young Solomon—who has seized the throne with the necessary despotic force—visits Egypt to help secure Israel's place in the world. There the backwardness of his people becomes all too evident to him, and the vision for a dynamic Israel is crystallized. The Pharaoh gives him a daughter, Khate, for wife. After he returns to Israel, Solomon builds a house for Khate, and his intelligent and charming wife comes to Jerusalem, thus permitting Fisher to keep the cultural achievements of Israel in constant contrast with those of a more civilized nation.

But if Solomon is a rebel with a cause, he is also portrayed as a man whose character hinders his program. He overindulges his appetites and is increasingly hesitant about taking action against his enemies—a noticeable contrast to his ruthless seizure of the throne. Although sympathetic to their problems, Solomon has trouble with his many wives. He unwittingly provides great internal opposition for his plans by bringing to the palace as concubine, Zeruah, whom he later marries. Solomon does not know what Khate soon intuits: the father of Zeruah's child is Ahijah, Israel's most influential prophet and Solomon's chief enemy.

The major irony of the novel is that Khate is the one who does most to uncover the court intrigue. She sounds out Zeruah, her son Jeroboam, and Ahijah; and she is most aware that Israel needs a clearly established policy for succession to the throne. But, fittingly for Fisher's theme of the wifeless Yah, the woman's efforts are to no avail.

The many philosophical discussions which surround Khate's efforts are never dull. But though the main issues of Fisher's novel are clear and provocative, the story is not all it should be as a story. The pace is uneven, largely because the background to Solomon's reign is not solidly enough portrayed. Readers can grasp the legal and moral dimensions of his reign, but the economic background—the reality of the impending famine—is stated rather than demonstrated. Also, in the second half of the novel more time elapses than Fisher plausibly accounts for. Characters lament mistakes of the past, but the prime realities of the novel are the moments of philosophical discussion—and these do not lend themselves to a sense of much time passing.

In the next novel of the series, the handling of time, along with lengthy discussions, is again a major critical problem. *The Island of the Innocent* fails to achieve the force of *Valley of Vision* and is, fictionally, the weakest novel of the *Testament* because it is a curious mixture of the novel of ideas and the adventure story. Filled with intrigue, it is the story of the conflict between two philosophies of life giving rise to the Maccabean wars. Many characters complicate the intrigue, and we expect to learn more about the motivations of the major characters than we do. We also expect to see them developing as Wuh does in *Darkness and the Deep* or Gode in *The Golden Rooms*. However, Philemon, the hero of the novel, is a fairly static person; and his psychology is never very interesting or real, as that of

Fisher's Solomon is. A representative of the Greek way of life, Philemon is in love with Judith, a true daughter of Hebraic morality; but their love is not made completely plausible. Judith does undergo a major change, but Fisher does not make it completely convincing. The trouble is that, although Judith is no more bigoted than her sister Angela, who is on the other side of the ideological battle, she is much less womanly than Angela. Fisher has attracted our sympathies to the wrong woman. Their two brothers, Paul and Hosah, are also on opposing sides.

Fisher seems not to want to portray character so much as to symbolize that "the brother shall deliver up the brother to death, and the father the child; and the children shall rise up against their parents, and cause them to be put to death." Reuben—one of Philemon's best friends when the action starts, but an enemy who tries to kill him near the end of the story—is also more convincing as a symbol than as a person. The issues the characters debate in *The Island of the Innocent* are really what matters. But since their story covers some fifteen years, the reader expects character development. Besides, more than in any of the other novels, the seams with awkward transitions are too much in evidence. Background interferes too blatantly as Fisher frequently interrupts to present historical data, always a major problem for the historical novelist and one which Fisher—especially in his Americana—usually manages with more success.

The Island of the Innocent is, in some ways, like Hemingway's *For Whom the Bell Tolls*. Fisher's novel is, of course, researched history, and Hemingway's novel of the Spanish Civil War is a novel of contemporary history. Fisher's Philemon, though, is like Hemingway's Robert Jordan; he is a foreigner in a civil war in which neither side represents his beliefs. Yet in the war both men find their meanings and formulate more strongly their beliefs. Both novels are love stories: Philemon has Judith; Jordan, Maria. And it is important to both novels that the reader have a sense of what people are fighting for. Yet Hemingway, though lacking Fisher's knowledge and vision, concentrates his story with more skill. Hemingway packs his meanings—and several lengthy discussions—into three days, using flashbacks and the symbol of the bridge very successfully. Fisher depends on a more chronological arrangement and discussion, and the illusion of reality cracks under the strain. The intrigue and the pace of the discussions work against each other.

In *Jesus Came Again,* the ninth novel of the series, Fisher shows the immolation of the son before the stern Yah, and he portrays the savior-god concept as the result of the Maccabean decision for the Hebrew "Father" religion rather than for the Greek way, or a merging of the best of the two. That Fisher should attempt a Jesus story is not surprising, but that he should handle the most potent of the world's stories in a new way— make plausible to the skeptical temperament the most crucial events of the gospels without debunking them but giving them new meaning—is a considerable accomplishment. Fisher's story is tender, without being sentimental; and it is set against the background of the cruelty of a world which gave the masses a strong need to believe in a savior.

His hero is Joshua, who in some ways is more like Vridar than the figure of the gospels. He is a gentle man with no illusions of himself as savior; but, as the mass hysteria and agony work their power on his sensitive spirit, he gradually comes to desire self-sacrifice. Joshua is so portrayed that the reader is likely to feel the justice of the Cynic's declaration to the Greek woman Sirena: "There'll never be any messiah more genuine than Joshua"(103). Joshua was given rules rather than love by his mother, and he thus feels that he and the world about him need the love and sympathy of the mother. His own mother, concerned with following the letter of the law, knows nothing of the spirit. The whore Sybil sells herself to obtain food for Joshua and those who surround him—mainly women. And in her deed Joshua recognizes true female compassion. Like the biblical Jesus, Joshua finds that women sense in him a special kinship. They feel in him the magnitude of his message of love for all the degraded. Joshua is, like Fisher's Solomon, swayed by the female virtues which the prevailing religion of the desert has scorned.

The women who surround Joshua are of contrasting natures, and character interest is better sustained than in *Island of the Innocent.* The narrative is also more forcefully concentrated by the journey motif of Joshua and his followers in search of the messiah. The historical background is better integrated into that search, and *Jesus Came Again* has as well more moments of humor. Fisher subtitles this story, *A Parable*. As a parable it escapes the too large canvas of *Island* and also its complicated intrigue. And, of course, Fisher is telling his readers that the Jesus story rightly understood is a parable; Sirena tells Zillah when less questioning minds assert that the crucified Joshua has been resurrected:

> Don't you see that he has come—again? Can't you understand it now? He has come in the only way he will ever come—as he came a hundred or a thousand years ago; as he will come again next year, or a hundred years from now, or a thousand years hence. Don't you see? He has come, he will come again, he will keep coming, until in this world there are no more Lucias hunting for their lost children, no more soldiers with lances by dead men in the night. . ." (309).

IV *The Christian World*

Scarcely fifty years after the time of the birth of Christianity, the events which gave rise to it—as imagined in *Jesus Came Again,* or otherwise—were inseparably bound with so much myth that myth could scarcely be distinguished from fact. In the early time of the "Christian" world, a hero in the Vridar tradition, Damon, goes forth to inspect the origins of the dynamic sect; and his journeys to discover the source and meaning of Christianity comprise the novel of ideas, *A Goat For Azazel,* Fisher's novel of early Christian times. Damon discovers that the early Christians transformed their "Jesus" into a sin offering—into a goat for Azazel.

Plot in this novel is reduced to the barest minimum. Locale, too, is minimized. The novel can hold the reader's interest only as he is concerned with philosophical discussions about religion and Christianity or with accounts of the decadent Roman civilization. Major characters are only sketched, and we recognize them as shadows of the autobiographical Vridar and Neloa, Athene, and Angele. Fisher maintains that any novel rightly read is autobiographical, but throughout *A Goat* one can hardly fail to recognize Vardis Fisher's anguished search for an abiding faith. Damon is impelled by the demon that drives his creator.

Demon seems an apt metaphor, for too often the reader feels that Vardis Fisher is working and reworking his own quarrels with points of the Biblical narrative. While it is, of course, an adventure to share the results of Fisher's reading—for he has read much more widely than the vast majority of his readers— the technique of having Damon repeatedly ask questions when he already has the answers so that Fisher can bring in more of his reading makes the novel didactic with a vengeance. And Damon becomes crochety and a bore.

Alan Swallow suggests comparing Fisher's novel with Johnson's *Rasselas.*[2] Putting *A Goat* next to *Rasselas* emphasizes Fisher's failure to be selective enough and, in the second half of the novel, to vary the narrative pace. Johnson more successfully maintains a philosophic tone while giving variety to events. *A Goat* might also be placed next to a book Fisher has greatly admired, Cabell's *Beyond Life,* which contains the very minimum of dramatic frame. But again one feels the oppressive bulk of Fisher's novel. And where Johnson and Cabell maintain their bracing discourses with brilliantly polished prose, Fisher tends to be strident. He does not permit his characters to talk in a convincing manner because he feels compelled to cram too much in. Hence he overloads the novel with indirect discourse (something which hinders other *Testament* novels, such as *Valley, Island,* and *Jesus)* and speech mannerisms of the Vridar of *Orphans.*

But the contrast between *A Goat* and the novel which follows is a great one, for *Peace Like a River* is highly dramatic, even melodramatic. Damon and Ayla feared that the Christians would lose the real spirit of Jesus and ruin his story by taking it literally, and in *Peace* the Christians have done just that. *Peace Like a River,* the tenth novel of the *Testament,* is placed in the fourth century; Fisher subtitles it *A Novel of Christian Asceticism.* The story portrays Christianity quite literally as a religion of the desert, Ahijah's religion which rejected the lush valleys. Solomon had decried a Judaism of the "Father" and yearned for the warmth and joy of the "Mother." The early Christians also reserved their obeisance quite exclusively for the "Father" and went to the desert to deny the flesh.

Vardis Fisher's fiction has always revealed a strong sympathy for the female view, and *Peace Like a River* takes as its central narrative thread a defense of the female in a world men have made. It is, consequently, the one novel of the *Testament* shown almost exclusively from the heroine's point of view. The heroine, Helene, is a beautiful Antioch Christian (though really a representative of the Greek ideal of *Island*) who is kidnaped and placed in a brothel, a starting point which, though vividly rendered, is ultimately symbolic. Helene's fiancé, David, who is far from the conventional Christian because he questions, effects her rescue at the price of his own capture and deportation to a slave camp. Partly to atone for her "sin," Helene goes to the desert to see and live among the Christians who practice the severest forms of asceticism—although Helene discovers the passions of many are super-charged. One ascetic, Apollo, is willing to sign a pact with Satan in order to lie with Helene. On the story level, Apollo is as overwhelmingly a villain as Fisher has ever shown; but, rather than serving primarily as a melodramatic device, Apollo symbolizes the neurotic male ego which corrupts womankind.

The account of Helene's struggle with Apollo as she waits for David never lags. But, though the novel moves quickly, it is marred as art; for Helene does not always serve as a convincing mouthpiece for *Testament* themes. Not only does she swear in the Vridar manner, but she sounds too frequently like Damon-Vridar as she does when she talks with Apollo about his pact with the Jews:

"Why a Jew?"

He lifted his brows. "You don't know? Because Jews are accursed people and act as Satan's agents."

"I don't believe it. I've known Jews. Christians ought to be ashamed for the way they treat them."

"But the Jews are accursed. They rejected the messiah."

"They did not. Jesus was not their kind of messiah."

"You don't know how wicked they are. Did not Justin, the blessed martyr, say that no other people anywhere, or of any time, have been so guilty of wrong?"

"Does the fact that he said it make it so?"

"Justin was a holy man. Didn't you know it?"

With a smile that was almost a sneer she said, "I just don't care. And did you know that Christians generation after generation rewrote their gospels to make them more and more anti-Jewish? Do you know that some Christians three times every day in their prayers curse the Jews?" (149-50).

Occasionally in other characters Fisher interferes too blatantly with their existence as beings in the novel. A telling instance is the case of Thais, the most voluptuous prostitute of Antioch. In the brothel she disputes with too much sophistication to make very credible her conversion and her naïveté as a Christian.

Only at the end of the novel, however, is the story primarily discourse. Helene after two years in the desert goes with Mark, almost the only man who displays charitable motives, to Rome to observe the Council of Nicea. This quiet ending to a fierce story is also more properly considered on the symbolic than literal level. What Fisher points out through his brief account of the disputing Christians is that their doctrines do not have much importance in the light of the realities of the desert. The world still waits for the gentle Jesus, though Constantine has now proclaimed the empire Christian.

Peace Like a River, then, announces Christianity as the religion of the Western world. As a novel it brings a quickened dramatic pace to the *Testament* series, but it is not Fisher at his best. The symbols are overdramatized, and Fisher is too intruding in reaffirming certain doctrines. Thomas Chubb called *My Holy Satan*, the eleventh volume of the *Testament*, "history without shading,"[3] and there is a certain justification for application of his judgment to *Peace*.

My Holy Satan is, however, considerably more successful than *Peace* as a combination of the novel of ideas and the novel of action. Chubb's adverse criticism still has some validity, for Fisher puts his young protagonist, Richard, into contact with much more of the best that has been thought and said than the most fortunate scholars would have known in the thirteenth century. Granting Richard a nimble mind and great powers of retention, the reader is still likely to feel Fisher's historical overloading—fascinating as it may be. In his American historical novels, Fisher's characters live within more plausible lines of knowledge.

Occasionally the discourse of *My Holy Satan* is too conveniently set up for the sharing of Richard's knowledge and Vridar-like questionings, noticeably in Chapter XIII when Richard tells Hillel, the compassionate and thoughtful Jew who has befriended him, of his two months at Toulouse. Hillel keeps asking Richard, "What else?" and the like. At one point he says,

"All right, go on, get it all out of you" (161). But in the main, Fisher's novel of terror during the Middle Ages, when the church is at the peak of its secular power, has an intensity of action capable of bearing the intense discussion of ideas and a smoother narrative pace than the middle volumes contained. As in *Peace*, indirect discourse is minimized. The new concentration comes in part from a focus on fewer characters and on a changing protagonist.

One observes as a heavy part of the discourses of *My Holy Satan* the defense of the Jews that is so prominent in *A Goat* and *Peace*. Of course, anti-semitism is a notorious aspect of the Middle Ages, and treatment of the Jew in a novel of medieval life was almost a necessity for Fisher's scheme. Nevertheless, Fisher rather overcompensates for Christian persecution of the Jews by always putting the Christians in the wrong light, by making the demonstration of compassion almost the essence of the Jews—who, though they have many of the virtues Fisher ascribes to them, have not as a matter of historical record led mankind by universally championing the downtrodden. Nowhere does Hillel, for all his learning, observe the convincing lesson of *Valley of Vision*: the Jews chose to be a peculiar people, and Fisher's Solomon sees that the choice will mean that his people will be despised and rejected. Next to this decision, the fact that the Jews did or did not crucify Jesus seems almost irrelevant. Admittedly, the Christians have been very unchristian in their treatment of the Jews; and this terrible record should be in the *Testament*, but Solomon and Fisher saw why. It is unfortunate that Fisher in his zeal to rap the Christians lets the potent theme of the middle volumes fail to play on the scene.

In *My Holy Satan* the church of the Middle Ages is too often, despite the insights of some of its best minds, an instrument of brutality and a denial of the beauty of life. It displays the arrogance that Damon and Ayla in *A Goat* feared while they observed the infant sect. While undergoing the fierce agony of a heretic's trial, Richard realizes that his persecuters are, with a few exceptions, concerned for his soul. He saw the inquisitor as "a kind of angry and impatient and frustrated father, wearied by the stupid stubbornness of heretics who would blindly damn themselves to eternal torments rather than confess their errors and come to God. It was his duty and his unpleasant task to save them" (259). The female's position is as degraded as ever despite more subtle disguises of the chivalric code. The mother has still been denied freedom to exercise her healing balm.

In the face of the corrupt world which denies the beauty of the true religion of compassion and free intellect, there must be more Jesus figures, who through their brave adherence to his code of love and humanity sacrifice themselves to cast a little light in a dark world. Thus, Richard of *My Holy Satan* represents the orphan as savior. As the Western world has denied the valleys of vision for the desert; cast aside the mother for a tyrannical father; and, because of fear, missed the beauty of the human spirit, Jesus must come again to show man how to live with man and to demonstrate that the truth can indeed set one free. Richard's Jewish friend and teacher affirms for him this message in anticipation of their deaths and as an echo of *Jesus Came Again*: "I think Jesus is a symbol, a symbol of all good men who come to teach and die. How many times has he come and under what names? How many times will he have to come before mankind accepts his message?" (216).

V   *Journey Complete*

Richard's conclusions, of course, bring us very close to Vridar Hunter, who sees the world in a darkness at noon. Vridar asked, *What is man?*—and his look at the direction of man's religious consciousness caused him to abhor much of what he found. Puzzled by Neloa, Vridar asked, *What is woman?*—and he found that she was only what man had forced her to become. And as one brought up in a militant sect, Vridar puzzled, *What is a Christian?*—and marveled at what history shows. But Vridar's answers gave him a good idea of why modern man is where he is.

Many readers will disagree with Fisher about just where modern man is and with some of his interpretations of historical data. But any fair-minded person must recognize the honesty of Fisher's search; he must also respect the vast amount of scholarship that guided it. As well as exploring fundamental questions of existence, *The Testament of Man* challenges the modern world's noblest aspirations.

As works of art, the *Testament* novels must of necessity be less than the exciting scheme that gave them birth. They are also sometimes less than Fisher's best. Probably Fisher did the series too fast and paid a price for reading less fiction in his later years. Sometimes historical data overwhelmed the creator of novels. Like many of his characters, Fisher is sometimes impatient, which prevents him from making each scene sustained and vital. Yet the series, as a whole, is sufficiently varied to make even unnecessary repetitions forgivable, and the first two novels —*Darkness and the Deep* and *The Golden Rooms*—are as finely done as any Fisher has written. In the middle novels—*Valley of Vision, The Island of the Innocent,* and *Jesus Came Again*— Fisher is less even, but he often surprises by making the philosophic portions the most exciting reading. *My Holy Satan* blends the dramatic with the philosophic and symbolic with considerable skill. And, of course, the eleven novels make possible the powerful *Orphans in Gethsemane* which, if it is uneven like the rest of the *Testament,* is a provocative autobiographical novel; it is potent as the record of an alert mind observing a large span of this tortured century.

CHAPTER 5

Fisher's Essex: Antelope of Idaho

FISHER SAYS that his first published novel was in fact his sixth novel. No publisher wanted the others, and Fisher destroyed them as inferior work. When one considers *Toilers of the Hills* (1928) as a first novel, it is well to remember that the author had been laboring with the demands of good fiction for some time. The skill demonstrated in *Toilers* is more, therefore, than beginner's luck.

I *A Novel of the Soil*

Toilers is an important novel for several reasons. It is, first of all, vigorous in its own right because of the engaging characters, powerful descriptions of nature, a noble theme which escapes sentimentality and shows itself to be more complex than that of most novels dealing with the farmer's battling nature on the frontier. Critics immediately compared Fisher with Hamlin Garland, Willa Cather, Erskine Caldwell—without sensing that Fisher's range was more varied, more profound, and, in short, richer.

This novel is also important as the first significant fiction from the Rocky Mountain region to use native materials. It marked the birth of a new regional literature. Some critics thought Fisher was imitating, reworking old pioneer stories in *Toilers*. But he says he had never even read Garland and the American Naturalists who were supposed to be his masters. The facts are that *Toilers* is very different from those books and that it grew out of Fisher's own experience and his familiarity with his own country and people equally as much as did Faulkner's novels.

When *Dark Bridwell* followed in 1931, critics labeled Fisher an American Hardy and as such gave him enthusiastic response.

His region was, of course, the Antelope Hills of Idaho. Fisher admits he seriously considered an Antelope series.[1] As a start to that project he wrote a number of sonnets on Antelope people, most of which Fisher has since destroyed because he felt them too much in the manner of E. A. Robinson, a poet he greatly admires. Fortunately a few of these sonnets, including an impressive one on Joe Hunter, survive in two anthologies published by Caxton Printers.[2] While Fisher stopped writing poetry as a serious endeavor, he peopled his first four novels—*Toilers, Dark Bridwell* (1931), *In Tragic Life* and *Passions Spin the Plot*— with Antelope characters. All four were highly praised for their treatment of the harsh Idaho region. If we add to these the 1937 *April: A Fable of Love,* it is evident that Fisher had his own Yoknapatawpha County in mind. But Fisher's vision and the history of the time caused him to go beyond Antelope. He says, "the critics never understood that I loathed and hated the Antelope country and was merely trying to come to some kind of terms with it; so that I could proceed to another and more fertile area."[3] For Hardy, Wessex was fixed in its meanings but Fisher caught the American West in flux. Nor did his region have a long past, such as Faulkner found in the South, so serviceable for explaining the present.

Nevertheless the Antelope novels are a valuable contribution to American literature and are among Fisher's best. The Antelope country served his art well, and, in coming to terms with it, he disciplined himself better than in some of his later novels. John Peale Bishop, an important voice of the 1930's, felt that Fisher disciplined himself less and less as his tetralogy progressed, as he went farther away from Antelope. But Bishop praised all three of the books of the Antelope country (*April* had not been written and Bishop does not consider the short stories) and compared Fisher with the most significant writers of the decade.[4]

Toilers is also important because it anticipates the Antelope series. Although satisfying in itself, the novel indicates that Fisher was then thinking in terms of a larger work. One senses this in the novel's structure. The novel lacks plot in the conventional meaning of rising and falling action, but Fisher defines plot as conflict—and all of *Toilers* is a conflict. The conflict of this novel, concerned with homesteading in the dry Antelope Hills, is essentially that between the pioneer and nature. In place of the traditional rising action, turning point, etc., Fisher builds—which at first may seem merely the stock and trade of the Naturalistic writer—by the accumulation of vivid experience: the feeling, sights, sounds, smells of Antelope. But Fisher's method of telling his story makes the novel more than this. The novel has distinct rhythms, and these reinforce the theme powerfully.

The rhythmic effect stems largely from the handling of point of view. Although *Toilers* recounts Dock Hunter's struggle to make the dry soil of Antelope productive, the point of view from which the struggle is seen is his wife Opal's; and she also had her struggle. When the story starts, Dock, who is one of the first pioneers of the region, brings Opal to the lonely Antelope Hills. His brother Joe lives on the eastern boundary of the Antelope Hills in a bottomland, but Dock is the first to attack the hills themselves. Gradually other settlers follow, but for a long time Opal is neighborless. Dock goes to the valley occasionally, but Opal remains in her miserable hut. Lem Higley visits, and Opal listens to his talk with Dock about valley folk and the distant neighbors. Slowly Lem and Dock, with their stories—significantly often repeated—people the country.

Opal listens and gradually learns more about these people and ponders the drama in their lives. She repeatedly hears of big Hansie Hansen who cries like a baby that he has cancer while his pretty wife, Ella, openly wantons with other men. One day Opal hears that Hansie has miraculously changed and that Ella has reformed. Opal hears about Jad Thurgenstowen ("No man under the sun could swear as long and loud as Jad could" [70].); Jeff Weeg; Charley Wheaton, renamed Bridwell in the next Fisher novel; the mysterious old man who lives alone and never speaks to anyone; the ugly old maid Susan Hemp; Ruby Beal, the wanton school girl who helps shake the world of young Vridar; and Joe Hunter. These and other names play across the novel giving a sense of the passing of time and of the profound loneliness of Opal's life and of the Antelope Hills. Fisher says, "All these people Opal wanted to know, their strange ways and the loneliness of their lives" (216).

Fisher is also interested in all of these people, and he later tells many of their stories in *Dark Bridwell, In Tragic Life, April,* and in several short stories. He also introduces other characters who help give a vivid sense of the region. In *Toilers* their stories are only suggested, but with haunting effect as one realizes the grawing loneliness of the Antelope frontier. Much of Dock's teasing—repetitious and often loudly funny—reinforces these rhythms.

Toilers, then, sets up the theme of the whole of the Antelope novels in its rhythmic patterns: the loneliness, the isolation of the frontier. Like Vardis Fisher himself who said he hated the Antelope country and tried to come to terms with it through his books, Opal in *Toilers* tries to get over her hatred of it and finally does; but her victory is not joyous or complete. Opal's attitude is set against Dock's from the beginning of the novel, but the country even wears on Dock, and he confesses one day to Opal that he feels "a great and strange loneliness everywhere about, in no way alive as he knew life, but brooding over the hills" (59). Through dogged work and his endless clowning, Dock is able to conquer the feeling. But for Opal, the task is not so easy. Prudence Hunter (*Dark Bridwell* and *In Tragic Life*), like Dock, needs violent labor to keep her sanity in the Antelope bottomland. She finds Sundays almost unbearable since her religion forbids Sunday labor. Lazy Charley Bridwell is the one man to whom the country is ideally suited, but the isolation of the country destroys even him because it preys on his wife and breaks his family. June Weeg (*April*) finds her loneliness in almost double portion because she is very imaginative yet aware of the ugliness of her own life. The country also helps explain the story of Ella Hansen whom Dock and Lem discuss endlessly. Fisher says of her in "The Legend of Red Hair": "In the Antelope country Ella lived upon a hill in an old log shack. In summertime her yard sweltered in heat, in wintertime it was buried under the wild snows. She had no children, no garden, no trees. When she first came here as a bride she nearly went mad; in the long afternoons she would look around her and see only hawks and dust . . ." (*Love and Death,* 11). Ella is thus very like Opal, Prudence Hunter, Lela Bridwell—and very like Vridar Hunter.

Yet if Fisher hits mainly tragic themes in his Vridar story, he is able to display much of the rich laughter of Antelope in *Toilers* and to provide for future novels he had already planned a contrast to the even more oppressive life on the Joe Hunter bottomland. Like his brother Joe, Dock has a violent temper and

a streak of cruelty; but—unlike Joe—he can howl with laughter
and be exceedingly tender. In *In Tragic Life* Prudence reads
romantic novels to Joe. When emotions arise in him, he crushes
them; when Opal and Dock read the novels, Dock becomes
more tender.

John Peale Bishop thought that the novel to set beside *Toilers*
was *God's Little Acre*, and George Snell has sustained the tradition of comparing their elemental characters.[5] Ty Ty Walden of
the Caldwell novel searches for gold on his Georgia farm for
fifteen years, just as Dock tries to make wheat grow on Antelope.
Dock and Lem are amazingly ignorant, though Dock's ignorance
is sometimes merely pretense, and that alone makes him much
more aware of life than are the characters of *Tobacco Road*
or of *God's Little Acre*. Fairly typical of the light chatter in
Toilers is the scene in which Lem reports that Hansie Hansen
shot at the moon:

> "He hit that-air moon?" asked Dock, looking at Opal. "You
> say you see him hit it?"
> "With my own eyes, Dock, I seen him hit it. The first two
> or three shots he missed because he didn't have his range. Then
> he started pluggun it right off. Every shot would leave a little
> round hole like, that would close up. That moon is made a flame,
> Dock, and the hole would shut right up. But say, come over
> here. See all that-there black down next the center? That's
> where he hit it most. How far away is that moon, I'd wonder?"
> "How far away is that-air moon, Ope, do you know?"
> Opal gave them a long look of disgust and pity. She turned
> away to her child, but after a little she said: "It's too far away
> to be shot with a gun, I know that. I don't know how far away
> it is, but it can't be hit with no gun."
> Dock and Lem looked at each other. "Why, my God," said
> Lem, looking out again at the moon, "it ain't so far off, that moon
> ain't. You watch it when it goes down and you'll see it's right
> against the mountain over there. Why, it goes right around the
> earth, that moon does. . . . How far away is them stars, do you
> reckon?"
> "Some of them stars is only about far as the moon," said
> Dock. "The evenun star ain't enough more far to say about."
> "That's what I think, Dock. They're smaller, that's all."
> "I figger a man mighten take a cannon and shoot that-air
> moon right outen the sky. That would be a sight worth lookun at."

"I guess you think," said Opal pityingly, "I guess you think that moon don't light the whole earth. It just lights this ugly hole you call Antelope. It don't light the world thousands of miles south of here and thousands of miles east and west."

Dock and Lem again looked at each other. Said Dock: "I guess she's busted your figgers in two. Mebbe he didn't hit the moon a-tall."

"And that moon," Opal went on, "ain't made out of flame neither. I don't know what it's made out of, but it ain't flame."

"Why, of course it's flame," said Lem. "Did you ever hear of a thing give light what wasn't flame? It's a fire, that moon is. Just like that sun's a fire and all them stars."

"It's got to be a flame, Ope, or it wouldn't give no light. What's the matter of you anyway?"

"Not a thing's the matter with me. But that moon ain't flame. I read once what it is, but I don't remember that neither. But it ain't flame."

"Then how does it give light?" asked Lem.

"I don't remember that, but it ain't flame. Didn't you never hear of mountains on the moon?"

"Mountains on the moon!" cried Dock. "God amighty, Ope, don't be a plumb fool."

"Now that I study more deep in the matter," said Lem, "I see we ain't got it all figgered out clear as I thought. I can see that I'll have to think more about it. But he hit that moon, Dock, or I been a-drinkun too much coffee. Why, God all Friday, I could see the holes them bullets made!" (76-78).

The big differences between Caldwell's characters and Fisher's is the pioneer drive that Fisher's have, but they may also have simply greater intelligence. Caldwell's characters are victims of an economic system which has impoverished their soil, but they are hardly aware that they are in any sense victims. They are incapable of suffering as Opal or Mary Hunter suffers. The greater suffering and intelligence of Fisher's characters invite the reader to fuller participation in their world than in the world of Caldwell's "poor whites."

Joseph Warren Beach sees in the sexual hunger of Caldwell's characters a form of spiritual hunger.[6] The sex motif is greatly minimized in *Toilers,* but one doubts that human sex alone could adequately portray the pioneer's drive. Rather, Fisher makes the pioneer's struggle believable by showing that it is a constant protest against the almost crushing sense of frontier isolation. Ty Ty keeps digging—quite casually— for gold, and is never defeated, but never wins. Dock, however, conquers the land, but he realizes all the time that the pioneer struggle is a defined one—it is man versus nature:

But why, asked Opal, after deliberating all these things, why did he not use aspens for posts? They were easy to get and they were lovelier to look at. But aspens, Dock said, would rot off in a short while, even if cut in winter time. They were the most worthless of all the trees God had made. Cedars were good trees, and maples and red pines; but aspens and cottonwoods weren't worth the sod they grew on. God might as well have made good trees instead of poor ones, nighthawks instead of magpies, dragon-flies instead of ants, and elk and deer instead of skunks and coyotes. "Without I could a-made a better job of this-here world, Ope, why, I'm a plumb fool to speak about it. Some says we can't understand God's ways and God made all things for the best. Mebbe that's so, but I can't see it with the eyes I got now. I tell you what I think. I think things ain't turned out the way God figgered. I think things is just a-gettun away from God's control, that's what I think. And if you'll give your mind to it a little bit, why, you'll see I'm right" (67-68).

The themes of *Toilers* are repeated on different levels so that the narrative pace is nicely varied. Since intelligence is greater in Fisher's world than in Caldwell's, individual experience counts for more. Opal, for instance, thinks of the obstinance of nature in different terms from Dock:

Everywhere between the wide lonely sky and the rolling reach of this desert country were men, invisibly grim at their work, tiny things lost here and there among their efforts, scarring the gray breast of the earth and sending up clouds of dust. And this drama, when thus seen from afar, seemed to her no less absurd than hopeless, seemed like the drama of ants trying to build their kingdom in a plowed field. For she had seen ants working eagerly, week after week, carrying tiny sticks and leaves and bits of earth and building for themselves a home, and she had seen Dock come with a plow and bury their kingdom or scatter it in ruins. And she had seen the frantic survivors, building again for weeks or months with their tiny and invincible courage, and she had seen Dock come with a harrow and scatter them again; and again she had seen them build. And somehow, vaguely but certainly, the way of men here was the same, a mightier and more terrible power over them, but under their feet the same treacherous shifting of death. The way was the same. In both there was the awful shuddering uncertainty and there was the slow pitiless creep of ruin (252-53).

The story belongs completely to the characters Fisher created. Caldwell has been greatly praised for keeping his social criticism in the background, for presenting it through his characters. Fisher has frequently been condemned for keeping himself to the front. Yet there is no preaching in *Toilers*. The social criticism is subdued and is as much in the background as in *God's Little Acre*.

Toilers is most poignant in its presentation of frontier isolation. The narrative technique, point of view, vivid descriptions of the land, the accents of pioneer speech combine to make the novel a realistic, sensitive rendering of pioneer experience. As the first significant fictional utilization of Rocky Mountain materials, it suggests possibilities for a permanent literature from America's last continental frontier. It suggests an imagination teeming with other good stories to tell.

II   Dark Bridwell

The Antelope novels are themselves abundant evidence of Fisher's versatility. He is a Naturalist, yes; but he is not one who keeps working the same formula. Although it is profitable to group the Antelope novels together in order to see not only how large are the number of rich characterizations with which Fisher has peopled an area but also how all the books play upon the pioneer theme; it is also necessary to recognize how different the novels are. Each has a different narrative technique.

We have seen that *In Tragic Life* and *Passions Spin the Plot* function as a part of a great symphony and that *Toilers of the Hills* moves with rhythmic force but lacks conventional plot. In *Dark Bridwell* Fisher tries his hand at manipulating plot in the more conventional sense. The novel contains a single action: how Charley Bridwell isolated himself for a life of philosophizing and how his own character finally destroyed his empire. The action starts with the arrival of the Bridwells to the wilds along the Snake River across from the Hunter ranch. The rising action establishes the main conflicts with the family: Lela's loneliness and inability to reconcile Charley's tenderness and cruelty;

Jed's hatred of his father and his love for his mother. Jed hates his father for his cruelties and has promised to kill him. The turning point comes when Bonnie Adams visits the ranch and whets Jed Bridwell's appetite for the world beyond. He leaves home after Bonnie departs, and Charley's happy home rapidly disintegrates. Jed returns years later when Lela can no longer bear Charley and life in the wilds, fights Charley, and takes the rest of the family away.

The novel is in three books, one for each of the principal forces: (1) Charley is the mover who sets up a kingdom; (2) Jed commits reckless deeds and upsets the balance of Charley's life; (3) Lela ends her passive life and tries to remake it in the image of the tireless Prudence Hunter. Charley, Jed, and Lela were all riddles to the Antelope people; and Lela, the darkest of all. For them the book is named *Dark Bridwell.*

The point of view in the novel underscores that their lives were riddles, for the story is external: someone is trying to make sense of Antelope legends, and the narrative always reminds us of this. The opening sentence of Book I is: "Charley Bridwell, it is said his name was Francis, but that he detested it and took the name of Charley when he was still a youth—was six feet tall, florid and fat." The Bridwells' lives became legends, the main events of which are clear; and, in the novel, someone sifts the legends. The narrator reports that a particular number of events preceded the action, a device used more effectively in the tetralogy. Also, as in the tetralogy, the narrative continually speaks of a "later time."

This narrative technique gives the story an overriding sense of inevitability, of fate. Charley's life can only lead to tragedy and finally to great irony. Charley wanted to escape the drudgery of the world, the futile efforts of getting and spending. He also wanted to isolate his family from the sin of the world, to live the good life. Finally his wife forces the drudgery of the work world on him. His children hate his wild kingdom, and Charley finds that his daughter has played the fool with a no-account (and Charley does not face her pregnancy with wisdom); one son has threatened murder; the two older sons have left home. Charley's philosophy has been as unbalanced as the life of drudgery of the Joe Hunters, and the narrative technique anticipates the final disintegration of the "philosopher's" paradise.

The story, an engaging one, makes extremely vivid the wild country that haunted Vridar. Its portrayal of the violence of the Snake River gives added meaning to Vridar's hatred of it—and incidentally Vridar makes his first appearance in fiction in *Dark Bridwell*. The country is as much a force in the action as is any of the characters. All of the Bridwells except Charley hate it, and even Charley is distressed by the Snake River, for he sees in it the insane journey of unrest to nowhere. He prefers a calm stream. In the river is the secret of Lela, who wants to take her place in the affairs of men. Jed, like Vridar, hates the walled-in solitude, and it causes him to commit reckless deeds which intensify the conflict with his father.

In *Dark Bridwell* Fisher has added some memorable portraits to his Antelope gallery. Each of the three sections gives life to the person for whom it is named. Since Charley's philosophy gives form to the book, his portrait looms largest. Readers are not likely to forget Charley's clowning, the cruelty that is often a part of it, nor his devotion to his wife. The most frequent response of people to Charley is to like him immensely. Almost all on Antelope do—despite the fact that Charley is always "borrowing." Even Vridar in *In Tragic Life* finds Charley's rascality appealing, but Vridar's tortured view of life prevents his entering into Charley's fun. Jim Thompkins is twelve when he meets Charley, and, unlike Vridar, he enters immediately into Charley's deviltry.

And Charley's pleasures do sometimes take cruel turns. At one point he throws his sons (before Lela's eyes) into the raging Snake River in order to teach them to swim. He also likes to frighten the unwary, to humiliate them. He lives to regret a trick he perpetrated on his future son-in-law, who retaliated years later by ruining Charley's daughter's life. And Charley is sometimes deceitful, and his deceit leads to an even greater regret. After Jed and Thiel have left home and Lela has undertaken to make the farm pay, Charley—realizing his failure in rearing his sons—attempts a new way with young Ham. Ham is three when Charley teaches him to swear and chew tobacco. Lela is horrified when she discovers this, and Charley's teaching of Ham is the mistake which finally causes him to lose Lela—one of the things he had guarded against by coming to Antelope years ago. Nevertheless, in his mistake with

Ham, Charley has been pathetic. Years later Lela must have realized more clearly his motives and that in even this act there had been love.

There is a good deal of Charley in Jed, but in Jed the redeeming features are less prominent. Fisher ably shows why Jed became an Antelope legend in his own right. Jed revolts against the solitude of his home by becoming, as Fisher says, "an artist matching his wits against those of man and beast" (152). The region along the Snake River where the Bridwells live was once known for its rattlesnakes. After Jed wages war on them, not one is to be found. In all of his escapades, Jed—not his older brother Thiel—is the imaginative force. Jed early opposes his will against Charley, and Fisher shows enough of Jed's actions as a boy to indicate that Charley has a worthy opponent. Fisher makes believable, too, the fear of poor Vridar Hunter for Jed, the fearless menace from across the river.

Against the violence of Charley and Jed, Fisher places the haunted spirit of Lela. Both Charley and Jed love her, but she is powerless to understand either. For years she wonders—and tries to live with their riddles. Antelope folk wonder about her sanity. Near the end of the book the emotions which have been knotted in her break loose. Fisher has suggested her loneliness in several ways: her feelings for the country, her quiet clinging to Charley, her concern for her children, and in the concern of others for her—especially that of Charley and Jed. The Hunters across the river also find her especially appealing, and from her Vridar received one of the few kindnesses of his youth.

Thiel, Beth, and Bonnie Adams, the experienced young girl who wins Jed's heart, are all well done. The childhood scenes of the book are eminently successful. Though the substance of *Dark Bridwell* may be less than that of *Toilers* or of *In Tragic Life*, it is a controlled, balanced story which holds the imagination. Its characters are not easily forgotten—nor is the wild country which is their backdrop.

III   *A Fable*

Critics started analyzing Fisher by comparisons with Hamlin Garland and Caldwell, then with Dreiser and Wolfe. But Fisher was a novelist who would not stay conveniently labeled. The

VARDIS FISHER

1937 *April: A Fable of Love* was in a completely different vein,
and critics likened it to the fantasies of Robert Nathan and of
James Branch Cabell. *April* was indeed different from anything
he had yet done, though clearly it has the same sensitive feeling
for the country and the people of Antelope. One feels the same
penetrating mind commenting on the realities of life that created
the tetralogy and the other Antelope novels.

April is a fable, a short tale, about half as long as *In Tragic
Life*. It has little of the ferocity, the violence of Fisher's earlier
novels. Having seen his versatility in handling more masculine
aspects of the frontier, we recognize that *April* is one more
proof that Vardis Fisher is a Naturalist who is different. In the
more delicate *April,* he is still the explorer and rests his fable
in reality. Its meaning is found in the mind of June Weeg,
from whose point of view—except for one chapter—the entire
novel is presented. Consequently, a good deal of the novel is
more poetry than prose; for June's soul is that of a poet, and,
possibly excepting Vridar, she has the keenest imagination in
Antelope. Antelope is much more for her than dust and drought:

> And mountains she loved, too, with their stupendous shoulders,
> with their backs to the stars where winds poured over and
> spilled. The sky also was a wonder of color and curve. The sun
> laid its burning path from east to west or clouds heaped their
> masses of wrath and spoke in thunder and flame. Or a deep blue
> veil would spread over all, a vast blue tenting all living things
> and coming down softly to the skyline; or a blue that was
> mellow with golden glows and mists; or a blue with the sun
> in its inverted bowl like a melon of fire. . . . And clouds, too, and
> winds: they were full of unpredictable mad designs. They could
> be politely cool or they could be cyclones of insanity and wrath.
> Sometimes a wind was full of moanings and prayer or some-
> times it rolled across the sunlight in shimmering valleys of
> peace. . . (15).

June Weeg's imagination is so active because she has needed
something—some dynamic illusion, as it were—to make her life
on Jon Weeg's lonely farm bearable. Her mother, Kitty, is a
stupid, fat woman who sits around the house reading and re-
reading romantic novels, and by such indolent stupidity makes
her husband's absences frequent. June's biggest barrier to a
happy life is her ugliness: she is "a perfect hunk of homeliness"

[110]

(165)—short and dumpy; her only redeeming physical feature
is her smile. She has had only one real suitor, Sol Incham, and
Sol is the homeliest man on Antelope. June will not have him
because he is not a dynamic lover and because everyone in
Antelope expects that these two homely ones will marry. So
June lives a life of dream, picturing herself not as homely June
Weeg but as lovely Miss April. She waits for someone exciting
to rescue her from her dreary life. The irony is that June, who
sees how stupid is her mother's devotion to book heroes, keeps
telling Kitty that life is not like that of books.

The slight action of the fable turns on the arrival of William
Wallace Argyll to the Weeg ranch as a hired hand and on
what June does with this event in her imagination. She wishes
to change the pattern of her life—to make exciting possibilities of
the imagination find an intense reality—to make, in short,
Willie love her. Willie might prove more likely to love June
than the Antelope men, for he is not from Idaho and writes
poetry. He is as educated as the men in Kitty's novels and
just as proud, disdainful, and—June realizes—as ridiculous.

She does not, of course, get Willie to love her. Fisher's account
of her efforts makes delightful reading, for June realizes that
she will not succeed, that he is not worth much, and that she
is perfectly ridiculous. She wants to be an actress and to write
books, and she is an actress who is always aware that she is
acting. While Miss April performs or writes, June is always
around pricking her bubbles. And June's smile, we recall, is her
one attractive feature.

June does not accept Sol (who has tried to win her for eleven
years, since she was thirteen) because he is so prosaic. The
only thing she shares with him is a love of the beauty in the
world about them. But even his faithfulness to her she finds
rather stupid, and she dismisses him as a fool who is doing
good all the time to those in need. He is like another homely
do-gooder, Cyrano de Bergerac. If June could make him as
exciting as Cyrano, he would do; and one day she names him
Cyrano, companion to April. The function of Chapter IV, in
which the Mormons choose a bishop and the only time we
leave June's consciousness, is to show the reader that Sol is
not a complete fool. He is not a "book hero." He is bigger than
the pettiness of the community about him, and he has no

grandiose illusions about life. The once scandalous Ella Hansen, always an intelligent and now a chastened woman, tells the bickering Mormons the truth about Sol, and the course of the novel is to wait for the impetuous June to see it.

Her failures with Willie set her on the highly amusing trek of adventures which lead her to Sol. She visits the strange old maid Susan Hemp to discover the ways of old maids. One night she talks with Jon, her father, about his life with Kitty and the absurdities of Kitty's dream life and advises him to jolt Kitty into reality, never sensing that her relations with Sol are in ways parallel. Then, when June is overwhelmed by a desire to do something, she and Jon set fire to a section of land and watch the mad destruction. How, she wonders, is the fire like life, like love? From that night she rushes for new freedom. She dresses in a wild garb of roses as had a book heroine, and she gives Willie a wild chase in the woods that sends him from Antelope; she returns to the bitter Susan Hemp to discover that Susan loves Sol; she visits the beautiful Virgin Hill to discover her ways, and kisses her mouth; she tells Kitty she will become a whore; she seeks to discover the way with men from Ella; she walks five miles to a dance and only observes; she pretends gleefully with the man who picks her up along the way home and finally accuses the innocent, puzzled male of trying to seduce her.

June's frantic efforts are not merely the frustrations of an old maid. Her sense of irony pervades the book. She wants a wild fulfillment, for she has observed carefully what love usually means in Antelope. It does not usually mean fulfillment: it means baby after baby, hardship after hardship, and ugliness. June has had enough of ugliness. She discusses these things with Sol one day, and Sol—who senses possibilities for a deep fellowship in marriage if not wild fulfillment—rebukes her with a powerful grasp and savage kisses. He then wisely leaves and discontinues his weekly visits, giving June time to ponder his lesson. April dies when June visits Sol's empty cabin before her intended departure from Antelope, cleans it, prepares a meal, and comprehends the possibilities of a satisfying life in fellowship with him.

Fisher's fable shows that love is not overwhelming romance and that those who expect it to be so are likely to have a life of ugliness. But the moral of the fable is more than that: it also concerns noble illusions by those who have lives richly imaginative. Surely April's way is better than that of the bitterness of Susan Hemp, who says, "But you can't eat beauty, can you? Can a person live on beauty?" June replies, "I could—almost" (43). But she cannot. Her illusions keep breaking before her, and she is most unhappy. Later, when June rephrases Susan's questions to Sol, he can tell her the good of beauty: "To wonder about," he said. "There is no wonder in your oatmeal or your mattress, Juney" (65). Beauty must be based on an acceptance of realities, and with Sol, June is able to learn this and to take a way that is better than April's.

April is a delightful comedy with a quiet wisdom and, incidentally, is Fisher's favorite among his novels. That Fisher could write so delicate a story many critics found perplexing. But the poetry is also in the more masculine stories which preceded it. *April* was just one more promise that Fisher would be his own man.

IV Short Stories

Fisher felt that his major talent was as a novelist and not as a short-story writer. He felt he needed the broader scope and freedom of the novel form. Nevertheless, he has published thirteen short stories, now collected and presented with fragments from six of the novels in *Love and Death* (1959). Significantly, most of the stories were written during the 1930's, and seven of them—the best—are set in Antelope. The other stories share with the Antelope stories, however, Fisher's deep sympathy with the lonely and frustrated. Quite naturally, one thinks of Sherwood Anderson's tortured souls. Like Anderson's, Fisher's stories catch the lonely in those moments which suggest a meaning beyond the simple events described.

The non-Antelope stories do have their interest, but the characters are less intense. Mr. Graham ("Mr. Graham Takes a Bath") is almost any small businessman, and Fisher usually looks at the type rather pityingly. "As Death Is Lonely" is, like the Graham story, half satirical and half psychological. "The Rape of Linda" and "Odyssey of a Hero" are too exclusively thesis stories. In the former, Fisher tells the story of a mother who instilled in her daughter an extreme fear of—and hence fascination with—sexuality. Fisher conceived of the latter story as an allegory. Narrating the return of a World War I hero to his hometown—any town—Fisher shows, by tracing the rise and fall and rise again of the soldier's popularity, how relative heroism is. But in both stories, Fisher's thesis is clear before they are half told and exposition is too dominant. "A Partnership with Death" is more subtle, better sustained, and more suggestive of genuine emotions. The slight "Martha's Vacation" is closer to the Antelope vein, for it has a poignant, tender humor.

Except for "The Storm" and "Charivari" the Antelope short stories were all written during the years when Fisher was writing the tetralogy. In two, the narrator is Vridar. In *In Tragic Life* one of the frightening memories of death in Vridar's childhood was the night Brig Murden visited the Hunter ranch and with an ax purposely killed a colt which had been born to one of his mares during the night. In "The Mother," which takes place twenty-eight years later, Vridar, still haunted by this memory, finds employment with Brig Murden because he wants to discover the truth of the legends about this man. On the Murden ranch, Vridar is most puzzled by the eyes of Kate Murden, eyes of changeless dead expression. Kate has been cut off from all human fellowship. Later a mare again gives birth, and Brig immediately kills the colt. Vridar sees in the eyes of the mare the look of Kate Murden.

In "The Scarecrow" Vridar is working on the ranch of Jon Weeg. To keep away a stray horse who is eating the grain, the men build a fence. They find it necessary to add wire to the fence twice, and the third night the not-to-be-daunted horse is impaled on the wire fence. The men decide to kill the determined creature, but the bullets do not kill the horse. The men recognize a kinship with the determination and fight for life which characterize the horse. They devote their efforts then to the horse's recovery. After the horse dies, they tear down the fence.

One of the men who shared in these efforts was Joe Burt, who is as simple as June Weeg is imaginative. In "Joe Burt's Wife" Fisher portrays Curt Obbing's cruel jokes over finding Joe a wife. Curt is also in "The Scarecrow," and his is the voice which brings a climax in the affairs of Ella Hansen and Con Wote ("The Legend of Red Hair"). Curt had once suggested to June Weeg a naked dance in the woods.

In his Antelope short stories, then, Fisher portrays many of the characters present in the Antelope novels, persons who—like Susan Hemp of *April*—were also subjects of sonnets in the *Antelope People* sequence, or possibly would have been had Fisher not abandoned the project. Like Faulkner's characters, the Antelope people would probably have grown from work to work and taken on new complexity, for with just the Antelope characters we have—in the novels and short stories—Fisher's regional fiction is richly peopled. The characters are lively, colorful, and speak in Antelope accents. The creation of a fairly large number of engaging characters suggests indeed an important literary talent.

The Antelope novels and stories also reveal a writer experimenting with narrative technique, with point of view and plot presentation. The range is considerable, and the results provide much worth-while reading. Most of Fisher's major themes—especially since these novels and stories include part of the tetralogy—are present in the Antelope work. And in this regional fiction, Fisher holds the didactic to a minimum.

The short stories build on the image of a scenic background that the novels create, rather than adding to it. But Fisher's success in creating a beautiful, haunting background for the Antelope novels is tremendous. When one reads them, it is difficult not to be aware of setting, for one is always invited to imagine the wild country that haunted Fisher. The descriptions are probably most moving in *In Tragic Life* as we realize how much of Vridar's tragedy the frontier setting causes. We learn that the frontier is indeed lonely:

> He did not know, he never realized until long afterward, how his prison-home, with its variety of habits and moods, of wild passions and humors and secrets, entered into his blood and heart. He thought he hated the place, and he did; but even so he threw himself, time and again, upon the naked ground, feeling that within it lay the only friendliness, the only peace. He tried to hug it, to melt into it, to get hold of its great serene strength. He endowed trees with its power, and two of them, a huge pine near the house and a stately cottonwood in meadowland, he came to love, almost as if they were his kin. And when a storm swept over, making of the cottonwood a pile of green boughs and a trunk of riven flesh, he went off full of sadness and wept.

Because in this earth, loamy and sweet and deep, and in all the wonders growing out of it, he felt a personality not unlike his own. This home was called the ranch; but it was never the ranch for him. It was the center of the universe, with all directions leading from it; and so strongly did he sense this that when away, he felt out of bounds, uprooted, lost. He thought of himself, when in Annis, as being thirty-two miles from his life's center; and when in Poplar, sixteen. And in later years, after he had travelled far, he felt himself always as one on a circumference, so many miles from his life's root and core (381-82).

CHAPTER 6

Americana

VARDIS FISHER'S greatest fame and financial reward have been won as a writer of historical novels on American—particularly Western—themes. Because of his birth and his training in frontier Idaho, Fisher has been especially equipped to write convincingly of the settlement of the American West, and he has made the first significant contribution to the historical novel of the West. Henry Nash Smith's *Virgin Land* (1950) recounts the largely futile attempt to express adequately the Western experience. Writers usually failed because they were either exploiting Western themes, as in the Beadle "dime novels," or they were bound by the Eastern aristocratic codes which were the staples of Eastern fiction but had little place in life as it was being lived in the West. From J. F. Cooper on, writers were, naturally enough, Eastern oriented. Those who knew the Western approach to life usually had little time or inclination for writing.

Fisher, born on one of the last American frontiers, knew nothing other than the most primitive conditions and view of life. He was not far from wild animals, Indians, or relatives who told of Indian killings. The women who lived around him were not veiled, virginal dolls; neither were they Calamity Janes. They were the hardy stock that came to Idaho to settle, Mormon pioneers, the kind Fisher wrote of in his most famous novel, *Children of God*. The men Fisher knew were tough, usually ready for a fight, and hard workers. Though Fisher's American historical novels are very carefully researched, they have the added authority of one who knows well the conditions of which he writes. The man who could write the Vridar Hunter tetralogy and the first significant fiction of the Rocky Mountain region was singularly well equipped to treat the great themes of America's westward expansion.

To read these novels, as well as Fisher's regional novels of the Antelope country, is to be reminded how young our nation is and also to be amazed that our nation is still very much Eastern oriented. Fisher was born in a wild and woolly Idaho, where the first white child was born in 1837, the year Michigan became a state. But Idaho was a long way from statehood then because no one thought of settling there; it was a place one passed through on the way to Oregon. The land belonged to trappers and miners. Not until 1860 was the first permanent settlement made in Idaho—and that by thirteen Mormon families "who thought they were in Utah."[1] The world of young Vardis Fisher was very much the same country, and Americans can get a good sense of early pioneer life by turning to Fisher's historical novels.

The term "historical novel" covers a very large area, and the writers of such novels include men of very different views as to what it should mean. In college courses in the English novel, one usually first hears the term in connection with Sir Walter Scott; yet history, a sense of the past, is hardly the most distinguishing feature of Scott's novels. One has, instead, romance—all of the thrills of the old courtly romances now given enough concrete detail to fit into the new genre, the novel. History, for Scott, was background, and he was merely recognizing the pleasure people derive from escape into a time more picturesque and colorful, or seemingly less chaotic, than their own. Many novels since have built on this formula, and the result usually is to sentimentalize the past.

Fisher never looks to the past to sentimentalize it but to give as faithful a picture of it as is possible. His interest is in making the past come alive—not as it has been idealized but as it was. This does not mean that he bars bravery and the highest ideals from his historical novels—we have seen how his *Testament* values them. These traits are also in his Americana, but they are present because they were a part of the men Fisher carefully studied. Since the historian cannot make the past come alive as the novelist can, the historical novelist can most memorably present the real heroes of history, as well as the villains. Fisher's basic rule, however, is that the writer must not distort the past. How difficult obtaining an accurate picture of a man or period can be and how seriously Fisher has taken this responsibility, the reader can determine from reading his recent book, *Suicide or Murder?* (1962), a non-fiction work exploring the pros and cons of the alternative explanations for Governor Meriwether Lewis' mysterious death.

In his Americana, Fisher explored the possibilities for a new kind of historical novel, a method which enabled him to escape the peculiar distortion that increasingly comes into play in the *Testament,* where he also tried to present the past as it was but in part succumbed to the dangers of the didactic approach. Perhaps he did not fully realize the lesson of the method of his Americana, for they were written just before or simultaneously with the *Testament.*

I The Mothers: *The Novel as Chronicle*

One of the best of Fisher's historical novels is *The Mothers* (1943), and it illustrates admirably his technique in his American historicals. As is usual in his Americana, Fisher focuses directly on known historical persons and events; his method is to portray the emotions and feelings of people whose record he has studied, and lest he misrepresent them, he does not usually bring in minor characters of his own invention; the introduction of such characters frequently leads the historical novelist to distortion. *The Mothers* tells the story of the ill-fated Donner expedition across the Sierra Nevadas in 1846-47. The records of that expedition are plentiful, and Fisher saturated himself in them. There are, of course, mysteries connected with the trip, and, when the record is unclear, Fisher does not try to tamper with it. His method is that of a chronicler. He does not invent incident, just as he does not invent characters.

What he does is to tell the Donner story clearly and forcefully. He knows the country these people suffered in; he knows the record of their suffering; and he can imagine scenically their story. So he invents dialogue consistent with character as he found it in the record and he selects incidents which make the outlines of their story and his theme clear. For although anyone who reads *The Mothers* has the essence of the Donner story, Fisher has avoided a danger to which the novelist trying to present history as it was may succumb: the novelist may be so occupied with facts that he loses his story in detail.

The Donners had already suffered a good deal before we see them in Fisher's book, but Fisher takes them up in the midst of their fatigue and just prior to the most crucial tests they face. The reflections on human nature he wishes to make do not need the earlier experiences. What the reader needs to know of them Fisher shows convincingly and briefly in the consciousness of the poet-naturalist Charlie Stanton, with whom the novel starts.

Fisher is equally selective in his treatment of the most notorious and gruesome aspects of the expedition. He does not hide anything from his readers, but he does not exploit the cannibalism. He shows it as a necessary measure that conditions forced on the travelers; he makes believable their difficulty in overcoming the taboo, while suggesting that someone like Keesberg had no trouble eating human flesh. But Fisher's restraint is sensible. What a lesser novelist could have done with these incidents should be clear to anyone who has read George R. Stewart's authoritative non-fiction account of the expedition, *Ordeal by Hunger* (1936, 1960).

The Mothers, like all of Fisher's Americana, has an extensive or panoramic structure, rather than an intensive one. Fisher, a Naturalist, builds by the accumulation of detail. Yet he does not let his story drag, and for all of the sameness of the snow and starvation, he varies the tempo admirably. He sets human emotions in relief. The snow and death are always present, but so are the changes in human personalities. A distinguished example is Chapter Twenty-eight of Part II which shows life in the Breen cabin. Pat Breen lies in bed most of the time; while his wife does the family work, he reads his Bible and prays. He is not ineffectual: young Virginia Reed resolves to become a Catholic. Fisher uses Breen to ease the tension for the reader, as people like Breen lessened them for those in his party. Rascal that he is, Breen reads the less cheerful parts of the Bible, often selecting those parts he thinks will apply to his neighbors, and in his simple way he completely misreads Job and finds Job to be proud and impatient.

Alan Swallow has said that the Western story has two main virtues: action and human nature viewed "in simplified terms,"[2] which can be a potent combination as in Walter Van Tilburg Clark's *The Ox-Bow Incident* (1940) and in A. B. Guthrie's *The Big Sky* (1947). The effect of *The Mothers* is very similar to that achieved in Clark's novel. In *The Mothers* the characters suddenly find themselves cut off from civilization, and, trapped together, they realize more clearly what things hold them together and what human nature is. Like Clark's characters, they come face to face with raw nature and discover that they are a part of it. The veneer of civilization is pretty thin.

In neither story, however, do we find the conventional Western hero. Precisely because he rejects the romantic figure does Clark's story probe so deep into the problems of justice. In his researches Fisher found someone who might have been set as the hero in Bill Eddy, who was warm of heart and possessed the grit which makes heroes. Instead, Fisher's hero (or heroine) is collective; it is the strength of the mothers that preserved the "tribe." On the desperate trip across the mountains, even Bill fails; and Mary Graves, who must force him to break a strong taboo, finally becomes the leader. Fisher never lets his panorama lose its focus on the mother courage. In this two-part novel, part one ends with the completion of the journey across the mountains by seven of the fifteen who started; and Fisher does not follow the rescue but drops back immediately in time to the mothers at camp, and he keeps this focus always.

Some readers have found Fisher morbid and grim. They have felt that he has focused on the unpleasant side of life—and in a sense he has because he felt we do not understand this part of ourselves. We need to remember, also, that Fisher was from the frontier West where human behavior was frequently savage, and where passions of hate and greed were more dominant than we like to think. *The Mothers* reveals how grim the frontier could be. After the rescue party has reached the Donners at the lake camp, Cady and Stone get five hundred dollars from Tamsen Donner to take her children to Sutter's Fort, but they quickly abandon the children at the other camp. Another "rescuer" ransacks her cabin as well. To all of the suffering on the mountains, the greed of the rescuers is a terrible finale.

Fisher has exposed the baseness of human nature; but that quality is not his emphasis. He ends the novel not with Cady and Stone, but with gentle, efficient Tamsen Donner, who has displayed throughout the novel the spirit of womanly love, devotion, and strength. Her courage reveals a faith in human beings that makes the treachery of a Cady and a Stone less devastating. Moreover, the novel ends with Tamsen's refusing rescue in order to stay with her dying husband, for Fisher's emphasis is still on the mothers. His story is grim, but it is presented as a high tribute to the finer human ideals and courage. In a nuclear age, it is downright comforting.

II   Tale of Valor: *An Epic of Exploration*

Thematically, at least, the novel to be set next to *The Mothers* is *Tale of Valor* (1958), which recounts another famous trek across the American West, the Lewis and Clark expedition. While Fisher reveals the high courage of some in the Donner party, he is able in *Tale of Valor* to celebrate distinguished leadership, an ingredient so sorely lacking in the Donner expedition and the factor most responsible for the entire tragedy. Most of the travelers of the Donner party were Midwestern farmers who knew next to nothing about the mountains and the land they had to cross—and least of all about a wise control of a group of people.

Tale of Valor succeeds where other historical novels on Lewis and Clark disappoint, precisely because Fisher was able to penetrate more deeply into the minds of these great leaders and to dramatize their qualities of leadership against a backdrop revealing a firm grasp of Indian and frontier life. The difficulty of making a good novel out of the Lewis and Clark material stems from its being so constantly on the peak of high adventure and from its having implications for the new nation equally as tremendous. Mrs. Eva Dye tried to handle the material in *The Conquest* (1902), but her book can hardly be called a novel since it has no penetration of character, and none of the specifics necessary to create a setting.

The first attempt to make a novel of the great story was Emerson Hough's *The Magnificent Adventure* (1916). Although Hough purports to be telling the actual story of the expedition, he invents a great deal. He bypasses the actual adventure of the trip and makes the novel—and American history—pivot on an imaginary love affair between Meriwether Lewis and Theodosa Burr Alston, Aaron Burr's married daughter whose husband was very much alive. One suspects Hough found his material too vast and invented the love affair because he needed the conventional working of plot. Most readers today find the result rather mawkish.

Donald Culross Peattie picked up the story again in *Forward the Nation* (1942). He also found the material too vast and tried to give structure to a greatly reduced account of the journey with interweaving chapters set in France to heighten the sense of the political implications of the expedition. More than anything, his book is a lyric celebration of the great adventure; it is not a vivid presentation of the men who made it.

Actually, Ethel Hueston had given a much better account of the journey in *Star of the West* (1935), and her technique and spirit anticipate Fisher's *Tale of Valor*. She invents neither character nor incident; she relies on the journals of Lewis, Clark, Floyd, Ordway, Whitehouse, and Gass. Her book must give way to Fisher's, however, because Fisher better describes action and more vividly portrays the explorers and Indians. Though she sentimentalizes Sacajawea, Ethel Hueston is not squeamish; she just lacks Fisher's knowledge of the primitive life which makes his account more convincing.

Fisher, like Hueston, felt that to portray the expedition would be enough. His novel, like hers, is a chronicle of the journey; it lacks plot in any conventional sense; it is a panoramic novel which presents narrow escape after narrow escape, discovery after discovery, hardship after hardship. Frederick Manfred described the technique aptly when he said the novel "wrote itself through him [Fisher] more than he took it over and wrote it, but that's something he couldn't help. It's just a tremendous theme, epic in its own right; he couldn't tamper very much with it. But he did fill it out."[3]

This method has obvious risks. Fisher's novel is a long one, and readers may tire of the monotony of high adventure. But, of course, that is what life was like on the expedition and also the reason it has inspired so many imaginations. Fisher's epigraph to the novel quotes Coues: "The story of this adventure stands easily first and alone. It is our national epic of exploration."

But most readers will not tire of these adventures, for they are well told; more important is the fact that Fisher shows the qualities of mind of Lewis and Clark that make meaningful the excitement that pervades the book. The captains are hardly older than their men, but they know how to discipline them, how to earn and keep their respect; these interactions are convincing because the men Fisher shows are healthy and earthy. Because Fisher presents men who are men, his narrative has a great deal more humor than the other fictional accounts of the expedition.

The captains understand the Indians also, and Fisher's narrative presents the Indians with the same authority one gets from the journals themselves (a presentation different from the Indian so often portrayed). No little part of the expedition's success was the ability of Lewis and Clark to see into the Indian mind, which Will Clark continually reiterates is the mind of a child, and the journey shows that Indian courage is frequently no more than the pretense of a child. However, the conclusions the men come to about Indians who have been in contact with white men and those who have not is hardly flattering to the white man.

Fisher reveals throughout, the habit of mind of both men as adventure follows adventure. Clark is quieter and the greater realist. Most often the philosophical musings come from Lewis, as in the winter sufferings on the Rocky Mountains: "I expect the will to live is in exact proportion to the intelligence" (298). Burning throughout the novel is also a sense of the vision of the expedition, particularly in Lewis, who realized the political necessity of winning the Northwest for the United States so that the young nation would not be an easy prey for European powers. He realized the importance of the expedition for Jefferson's political position. *Tale of Valor* celebrates that driving vision which determined the growth and security of the nation. In convincingly portraying the leadership of Lewis and Clark, it celebrates as well the vision and leadership of Thomas Jefferson, who not only saw the political advantage of the carefully maneuvered—and of doubtful constitutionality—Louisiana Purchase, but who also knew that Meriwether Lewis was the man to whom he should entrust the leadership of an almost impossible undertaking.

III Pemmican: *A Novel of Indian Exploitation*

The specificity of Indian life that is one of the strengths of *Tale of Valor* Fisher had already used in *Pemmican* (1956), a novel which has at its heart the relationship—which Lewis and

Clark frequently ponder—between the Indians and the whites. In *Pemmican*, however, Fisher has no great epic, no great vision to celebrate. The novel is a presentation of the Pemmican War (1815-21), the conflict between Hudson's Bay Company and the North West Company for the Western fur trade. One looks in vain for the vision and ideals of the Lewis and Clark expedition in this war, for both sides wanted only profit and used unscrupulous methods to get it. Caught between the two companies was the Indian, whom both companies used unfairly. Yet both sides needed him: he provided them with furs and pemmican, the meat mixture necessary for the long winters.

Although *Pemmican* was very popular in Germany,[4] American readers found it less palatable. Objections to *Pemmican* stem from the pervading barbarity and sordidness of both Indians and whites. Of course, most readers are unfamiliar with the Pemmican War, for it had no immediate political consequences, and it was also Canadian. The war itself had no great climax and ended with the merger of the two companies; but the demoralization of the Indians was permanent—and was not restricted to the Indians on the Canadian side of the border. The companies had posts in the States as well. Men, such as those Fisher shows, are the "mountain men" who lived in Idaho before settlers ever came, who pushed into the Oregon Territory, and who helped to form the West—and to destroy the Indian. Fisher shows important background that formed their character.

The Pemmican War was not pleasant: so Fisher found in the record and so portrays. The *Encyclopedia Britannica* summarizes: "In the competition which arose between the companies the Indians were demoralized, body and soul, by the abundance of ardent spirits with which the rival traders sought to attract them to themselves; the supply of furs threatened soon to be exhausted by the indiscriminate slaughter, even during the breeding season, of both male and female animals; and the worst passions of both whites and Indians were inflamed to their fiercest."[5] Perhaps because the war was so lacking in positive values, Fisher, for the most part, abandoned the chronicle technique. The incidents and characters of *Pemmican* are mostly his own creations. Nevertheless, the outlines of the war are clear and accurate. The reader learns about the persons and the issues involved and, above all, their effect on the Indian.

But there is also an important biographical reason for Fisher's abandoning the strict chronicle method. *Pemmican* appeared in 1956, the year that Alan Swallow began to publish the *Testament of Man*. *Pemmican* reflects Fisher's attempt to get back into the public light. The prize-winning Western novelist wanted to remind readers of his earlier reputation, and an American historical seemed a worth-while gambit. Anxious to revive his reputation for the sake of the *Testament*, Fisher wanted *Pemmican* to sell. This desire would make less likely a strict chronicle approach to the Pemmican War. The way to a best seller is usually a love story; thus *Pemmican* is the only one of Fisher's American historicals to use a plot revolving around a romance. However, any popular love story was beyond Fisher; and the grim aspects of the Pemmican War made unlikely the revival Fisher sought. And Fisher was so immersed in the *Testament* that the story of the conflict of the Indians and whites shares the themes of the *Testament*.

Fisher presents his story essentially, but not exclusively, through the point of view of David McDonald, and it is his character that creates the novel. David, a young Scotsman who came to Hudson's Bay, found a country that changed his life and way of looking at life. He is strong, courageous, intelligent, but he is also romantic and sensitive:

> A half dozen times he had read *The Tempest*—of a certain island in a certain sea, of an old man named Prospero, and his daughter Miranda, so very lovely, like all Shakespeare's heroines. "Knowing I lov'd my books, he furnish'd me from mine own library with volumes that I prize above my dukedom." He was recalling now her words, "with my heart in 't; and now farewell . . ." He felt like that today. He foresaw more clearly he was sure than Jim, if not more clearly than Colin, the dark months ahead, the strife that would "run upon the sharp wind of the north" and "set a mark so bloody on the business"; and he was not sure that he would not meet his end in it. It was not too hard to die if you had known your woman, but it was hard if you had not known her and were still young. When Jim sent him out into the frozen winter he would be on the very spearpoint of danger and, unlike Prospero, no woman's nor any person's indulgences would set him free. It did no good compassed about with storms to try to decide what to do, nor in the chilled loneliness of his bed, nor when making pemmican or sitting

before a blazing fire. Shakespeare knew what it was that carried
a man to the tide's pitch, he know that once you were thrown in
you were a fool to buck the current if you hadn't the strength
for it. All his plays told you that. They all carried the same
lesson, that passions ran at far greater depths than reason, ran
in mindless darkness like that of slow senseless waters in moon-
less midnight (144-45).

In essence, David has a good deal in common with the autobiographical Vridar Hunter; but he is never so morbid, nor does
he preach his convictions so hotly. But, like Vridar, he is a man
of the mountains, who feels a kinship with and a love for wild
country. David's feeling for the country suggests Fisher's treatment of the Antelope region. But, more importantly, David is
concerned with the problems that torment Vridar—cruelty in
the human race and what makes a man civilized. Like Vridar he
finds the relationship between the sexes most telling in these
matters, which are central to Fisher's whole *Testament of Man*
series; and David McDonald might well have been a hero in
that series. After he sends One Ear back to the husband who
has just beat her

> He said to Pierre, "Send Payette along with some rum for him
> and tell him that if he beats his wife again he'll get no more
> rum." It was easy to say that and it was no good: when Latude
> got drunk he would beat her again and someday he would kill
> her. That was why a man hated trading with Indians, all the
> rum and drunkenness, the brutalities and murders and all the
> torture and heartbreak. It made a man wish sometimes that he
> had never been born (68).

Most of the traders are not very disturbed by the cruelty
about them. Or, if they are, they learn to disregard their feelings
—but not David. When he is a prisoner of the Blackfeet, he
interferes with their dealings with a captive Cree girl. In
revenge, a squaw has her little boy cut off David's thumb at the
joint. The other traders regard women—especially Indian ones—
solely as instruments for their pleasure. David can understand
the Indian's hatred for the white man, particularly the hatred of
the half-breeds, which finds such savage expression in the
destruction of the Red River settlement.

Because David is different and because Fisher had stressed in the *Testament* the need of men for gentle female love, David's attempts to win the love of Princess Sunday, a white girl brought up as an Indian, are not mere sensationalism. The love that develops surmounts fierceness, but is tender without being sentimental, nor is it divorced from the cruelties of the Pemmican War. The men who debauch the Indians do not have such love. When Jim Dugald is explaining to David what it is to be *"un homme du Nord,"* he says: "We're a different breed now. I don't know if we're better or worse. God knows we're different. I guess the chief thing that makes us different isn't the distances and the size but that we don't have women. I guess there are things women do for men that should be done for them, or they just don't go on being men" (48).

Jim has this insight because he once lived with an Indian woman named Tumtum. At that time he thought of her as less than human. "I can recall now so many ways she had trying to make me love her a little. A woman's ways, I guess they were" (42). Jim's and Tumtum's baby was born blind. One day he discovered Tumtum kissing the child's blind eyes and praying to the white man's God: *Pater noster, qui es in coelis, santificetur nomen tuum.* Baby and Tumtum died shortly thereafter. Tumtum's story preys on David's mind, and it echoes throughout the novel. Thus, the struggle for the food staple, pemmican, is symbolic and its meaning very like what Fisher was emphasizing at the same time in his *Testament* novels.

Pemmican, then, is an account not only of Indian ways but of white man's ways with Indians. It portrays them graphically— and for some readers too brutally. It presents them from a significant point of view, and with tenderness. But to quarrel about the novel because of the ferocity and the barbarity of the company and of the Indians is to criticize the record of the Pemmican War. If the novel is not excellent, it is because the love affair has more drama and mystery surrounding it than Sunday's half-tamed character or the already intense competition between the two companies merit—and Fisher divides himself between the two. The indirect discourse that increasingly hampers the *Testament* is just as harmful in *Pemmican*. It is hardly in keeping with a rapid dramatic pace.

IV City of Illusion: *Greed and Vanity in the American West*

In *City of Illusion* (1941) Fisher presents another dramatic aspect of his great theme, the exploration of the West. As the title suggests, *City of Illusion* is a study of an atmosphere, a time, a place: Virginia City, Nevada, in the exciting heyday of the Comstock Lode and of fabulous wealth. The discovery of silver there corresponded with the start of the Civil War, but the times were such that the miners barely took notice of the national conflict. A rebel supporter might take a shot at a Yankee supporter during the evening "opera," but this was not an event anyone particularly noticed. Men were interested in money and power or in raising hell, and almost all the women were prostitutes. Putting down an Indian uprising was immediate, but Mr. Lincoln's war was distant. The discovery of silver in Nevada would mean Lincoln would have Nevada admitted to the Union to strengthen his party and the nation's credit abroad, but Virginia City had little concern for anything other than its own extravagance—though much of its wealth was finding its way to the making of the greater extravagances of Nob Hill in San Francisco.

Fisher's novel—in the extravagance of its many episodes—frequently catches the spirit of the little camp that suddenly became a town, then a city that caught the eye of the world, and almost as suddenly a ghost town. Virginia City's story is unique because the silver wealth was concentrated in one spot, unlike discoveries in Colorado or California. Consequently, Virginia City was a concentrate of greed and lawlessness.

For the writing of his novel, Fisher studied carefully the facts and legends of Virginia City; he found there the main characters and incidents of his story. Again, his problem as novelist was not to invent, for Virginia City's history was exciting enough. Rather, Fisher needed some meaningful way to arrange the fantastic record. He chose to concentrate on the story of Eilley and Sandy Bowers, two comic but pathetic figures whose fortunes reflect the history of the whole city. The background to the novel is the struggle for control of the Comstock wealth. Enough of the struggle is in Fisher's novel to make the outlines clear, but it is never the focus. The Bowers only imperfectly understood the machinations that took their fortune, and Fisher tells only enough to let his readers know.

The Bowers' story has caught the imagination of many. (Mark Twain, a background figure in Fisher's novel, tells of Sandy's trip abroad in *Roughing It*.) Historically, there is justification for a focus on the Bowers. Theirs was the first great fortune to come out of Comstock, and they spent their money in such vulgar sprees in Virginia City and in Europe that they helped advertise their city to the world, encouraging the kind of speculation that made millionaires of the few who established Nob Hill and paupers of the many—finally even of the Bowers.

The Bowers with their huge mansion were catalysts (particularly Mrs. Bowers), and that is what Fisher makes of them in his novel, and from this he derives the novel's structure. Eilley desires not only wealth, but position. She wants to be queen of Virginia City. Her desires incite other women to push their husbands to outdo the Bowers.

The pattern of the novel changes only when Fortune suddenly drops those she has favored. Near the end of the novel, Eilley and John Mackay watch an eclipse of the moon from the mountain above Virginia City. Eilley has lost her fortune and John Mackay, once penniless, now wields the power of the Comstock. Mackay is unhappy with his wealth. His wife, who was jealous of Eilley, is in Europe. Mackay senses the emptiness of wealth and position. But Eilley has no sense of the vanity of her past. The whole city has been equally as blind.

The novel shifts back and forth between Eilley's ridiculous efforts to find happiness by making herself the leader of Virginia City society and the pathetic story of Luff McCoy. Luff, something of a philosopher to whom wealth means little, has a wife who finally goads him to seek it, largely because of Eilley; but he only gets into debt, and his wife leaves him. His daughter realizes he will never achieve riches. Scorned by Eilley and other "proper ladies," the girl establishes her power through prostitution. Luff, a contrast to Eilley, is Fisher's most moving statement of the human values that Virginia City lacked. Luff, despite Eilley's protests, is Sandy's friend; and in Luff are portrayed the basic ideals of human fellowship. After Sandy's death and after being forsaken by his own wife and daughter, Luff wanders in drunkenness at night on a mountainside and falls into a hole where he is trapped with a goat that has also fallen:

> His mind was clear now. He knew well that he was alone with a dying beast in a dark cold chamber of the earth and that he was dying too. He knew much more than that. There came to him a realization that seemed to be the meaning he had hunted for all his life. A goat was something a man could milk and eat, but it was also something that he could die with. This recognition of kinship, of the common destiny, from end to end of the earth, of living in loneliness and dying alone, seemed to him now the only certain meaning, the only unalterable fact, in all breathing things. If he had been lying here with another man, he could have understood no more and no less than he understood now (378).

This realization is beyond Eilley and most of Virginia City. Sandy tried vainly to hold on to his old friends, but Eilley and Virginia City were against him; they followed after an illusion and missed more fundamental values.

The characters in Fisher's story are fairly simple. Eilley is a little more complex than most of them. She is comic, yet has a certain kind of intelligence and gumption. She reaches out pathetically in her attempts for motherhood, for a larger fellowship; but her desire for position gets in the way of her common sense. However, Eilley and Sandy are too simple to bear the weight of so long a tale, and Fisher surrounded them with anecdotes of the wild life of the Nevada City. Like Wolfe, Fisher can be a great "putter in."

Fisher's novel is not so forceful, therefore, as his theme or his other Americana, possibly because he focused on characters whose psychology did not interest him enough. Fisher's heart was really in the *Testament* he was planning.

Nevertheless, the novel is informed and has some good scenes. Through it, one gets a vivid sense of a revealing chapter in the settlement of America.

V   Children of God: *The Mormon Search for Freedom*

The first novel in Fisher's Americana, *Children of God*, is in many ways the most significant. For one thing, it brought Fisher his one best seller as well as the Harper Prize ($10,000) for

1939. It also brought the frequent judgment that Fisher had written one of the best historical novels of the decade and that it was the finest treatment the Mormon story had yet received in fiction. Twenty-five years later it is still the most widely read of Fisher's books.

Not unexpectedly, however, the positive judgment which prevailed after the book's appearance (and which is reiterated in 1950 in Ernest E. Leisey's *The American Historical Novel*)[6] has not gone unquestioned; for one seldom finds agreement about any of Fisher's work. The Mormon church officially repudiated *Children of God*. This may be somewhat surprising since one of the most praised traits of the novel is its fairness. Carl Van Doren, who with Louis Bromfield and Josephine W. Johnson judged the Harper contest, praised the achievement in his *The American Novel 1789-1939* for neither exalting the Mormons nor abusing them.[7] Fisher obviously does not start with the basic Mormon assumption that God restored his church through Joseph Smith, but the Mormons may have been upset by the final movement of the novel which shows the Mormon church as setting aside much of its uniqueness and as taking its place along with other Protestant denominations.[8]

Fisher has also added to the *Children of God* controversy. He said it is one of the poorest novels he has written.[9] One suspects his view is, in part, a protest at being remembered as the author of a single book, which for some time seemed to be his fate. Then, too, he probably felt he could have written a better novel on Mormonism after he had made his extensive study of religious history, symbols, and myths for the *Testament* series.

Despite the Mormon church and Fisher's objections, however, *Children of God* continued to be regarded as a classic among American historical novels, and fourteen years after its publication, the novel was still influential enough (at least in Utah) for an article to appear which attacked its historical authenticity.[10] David B. Davis picks several quarrels with Fisher. First, he attacks him for attributing the birth of Mormonism to frontier conditions. Interestingly, in "The Centennial of Mormonism" Bernard DeVoto, who has studied the Western movement carefully, says that consideration of Mormonism as a frontier movement is the only intelligent way of studying it, and this point he stresses throughout his article.[11] In any case, Fisher indicates the conditions that prevailed in Joseph Smith's region, and Davis' argument is finally a pedantic quarrel over terminology. Davis further objects to Fisher's statement that Joseph had "humorless eyes." Davis cannot quite believe that Joseph was a mystic (nor, one assumes, then, that Joseph could deal with the mysteries of God). Again, DeVoto's characterization of Joseph—sensible if not a universally accepted portrait—indicates that Fisher was not being blatantly inventive or deceitful. Davis also questioned Fisher's treatment of the purpose of the exodus to the West. DeVoto says that Brigham Young was *probably* hoping to escape American jurisdiction and that Mormon feeling about loyalty to the United States was ambivalent and pragmatic. The fact is that the Saints were going to territory that was Mexican and would be so for two years. Certainly many of the Saints hated the United States government, and, as a novelist, Fisher had to make some decision on a debatable matter, but he did not violate American history. Finally, Davis castigates as most inaccurate the episode in which Brigham meets Jim Bridger and talks about Mormon prospects in the Salt Lake Basin. He here calls DeVoto to his aid, and one concludes that Fisher accepted too literally Brigham's good story (often repeated) about the meeting. The scene is not a long one in Fisher's book, nor is it crucial—or even memorable. The reader is not led very far astray.

So Davis hits upon one real inaccuracy, but he intimates that there are many more—and he fears that, since the book is so vivid and powerful, it will do real harm! DeVoto, though he says he read the novel slowly and critically, must have been drowsy; for he said *Children of God* places Fisher "in the small company of our best,"[12] not only because the novel is alive, but because it is factual—precisely, because it gives one a solid notion of that great American story. Even allowing for some exaggeration in DeVoto's rating of the book (certainly *In Tragic Life, Toilers,* and *Dark Bridwell* are more sustained), the reader will find his review carefully critical. Ray B. West's non-fiction *Kingdom of the Saints* (1957) also indicates that Fisher's novel is historically sound. The average American with only a high school or college survey in American history will know a good deal more about his heritage after he reads *Children of God.*

Fisher presented an interesting account of his preparations for writing the novel in a University of Oregon symposium.[13]

He had planned to write a novel on the Mormons some dozen years before he did one, and he read everything about them that he could. He resolved to tell the story as objectively as possible. During the writing, he kept books around him by Mormons and by their enemies, and he looked at them from time to time to remind himself of the middle ground he wanted. After the book was published, he recalled, some persons wrote to attack him for being unfair to the Mormons; others wrote condemning him for proselytizing for the Mormons!

General critical consensus, though not unanimous, was that he had achieved the role of objectivity remarkably well. Some critics expressed surprise that Fisher was capable of being so detached, of not preaching—though one suspects they had not read *Toilers of the Hills, Dark Bridwell,* or *April* or given fair treatment to *In Tragic Life.* Nevertheless, Fisher has no obvious mouthpiece in *Children of God,* as he had in *No Villain Need Be* or in *Forgive Us Our Virtues.* Mark Browe in the final section of the novel comes closest, but Browe's function is so integrated into Fisher's presentation of polygamy's crumbling under its own weight that the charge is unfair. In *Children of God* Fisher was anticipating the historical objectivity and concern with actual events that characterize the Americana to follow.

Fisher subtitled the novel: *An American Epic.* It is an epic in the sense of being an account of the journey of a brave people and of their establishment in a new land. It has many epic characteristics: great vision, battles, hardships, betrayals, defeats, victories, and at least one epic hero. All of this is to say that Fisher has attempted a good deal. The result is, of course, a vast panorama; and, since Fisher must treat so many persons and events, the result is not always so even as that of the simpler, more closely bound events of *The Mothers.* Occasionally he crowds too many events in a chapter and sometimes causes the reader to make too sudden a transition, but the whole is concentrated on the epic qualities of the Mormon story and succeeds in retaining reader interest.

Some critics felt Fisher did not do enough with the appeal of Mormonism, the message that won the hundreds of converts. Alfred Kazin wanted more of the Mormon idea,[14] but probably the most important part of that idea is in Fisher's novel and is worked out dramatically. The Mormon ideal is that of working out one's salvation, of *doing* for the kingdom of God—indeed of establishing that kingdom: hence, Fisher's emphasis on the epic. DeVoto also suggests that Fisher could have done more. He says that the novel does not make enough of Joseph's frenzies, explore the hysterias which resulted from them, nor present clearly enough the Mormon smugness which added greatly to their persecution. Fisher, in his attempt to keep a middle ground, may have omitted these wisely; and, as DeVoto acknowledges, the objections in view of the rigorous whole are minor.

Even Ray B. West shied away from the beginnings of Mormonism; his book starts with the church in Kirtland, Ohio. Other novelists using the Mormon material also dealt with the later phase. Doubtless, a portrait of Joseph Smith is not as easy to create as one of Brigham Young. But as his title indicates, Fisher is to tell the story of a people, and their beginning is with the vision of a fourteen-year-old boy in 1820 in Palmyra, New York. The first third of the novel, entitled "Morning," centers around Joseph and ends with his martyrdom. Fisher suggests psychological causation for Joseph's behavior, but he never posits psychological dogma. He presents a prophet who firmly believes in what he says—with only a hint that now and then he is consciously crafty. In the main, his Joseph has dignity. He is not without intelligence; and, as persecutions against him mount, he even becomes admirable. The scene in which he is tarred and feathered is so graphically done and Joseph so conducts himself as a prophet should that the loyalty of his humble followers is quite plausible.

Of course, Fisher presents Joseph as also bungling a good deal of the time. Joseph the dreamer did not always see where his plans would lead, but he knew how to conduct himself under persecutions—and Fisher is at his best showing them. More than anything, the persecutions united the Saints; without them, it seems likely that the church would have been choked from within, for there were apostates enough. As "Morning" draws near its end, Joseph is in great trouble because of his revelation over celestial marriage. Brigham tells him that the doctrine will be their downfall. In a response so typical of Fisher's portrait of the prophet in trouble, Smith says, "Brigham, is your faith weak? What God commands, we do" (273). To non-Mormons Brigham's insight is less reprehensible. More than anything, Joseph's martyrdom saves the crumbling church, for the church had had enough of revelation and needed a leader to guide it. This section ends with a vivid presentation of the martyrdom, and Fisher's epic pauses to leave the reader to ponder the American conditions that had forced a people who wanted to serve their God to flee from Palmyra to Ohio to Missouri to Illinois and finally to a territory outside the United States.

Section two, entitled "Afternoon," is the story of Zion at her greatest, ending with the death of Brigham Young. The ground here is in a sense more certain for Fisher since he needs to deal less with visions and prophecy. Joseph had already given the vision, a kingdom for God's people, though Fisher has it more clearly defined for Brigham than for Joseph:

> He felt that this journey fed from the eager and searching millenniums in the remote background of human striving: it was more than desperate flight from enemies: it was a pilgrimage toward freedom, toward a fuller and richer destiny for the entire human race. In all its suffering and patience and courage, it was a mighty symbol of that struggle for perfection and peace that had been the heritage of humanity for centuries. He was fighting for a society that would be charitable and righteous and free (427).

Of course, comparison of Brigham with Joseph is inevitable, but Fisher leaves it for the reader to make. Whereas Joseph was often impractical, Brigham knew men (neither understood women very well—though Brigham slowly learned), and Fisher is repeatedly convincing in giving a sense of Brigham's firm leadership. With the Saints divided and uncertain after Joseph's death, Brigham deals as wisely with the Illinois officials as anyone could, and he leads his people into the far West to Mexican territory. Fisher says "the journey came overwhelmingly through all five senses"; but hunger, cold, stench, ache, illness, death could not long daunt the Saints with Brigham commanding. Brigham is often plain tough, but the Saints make it to the Salt Lake Basin, and there he oversees the building of a city and makes the desert bloom—only to meet again old enemies from the United States and, one feels, to meet them with wisdom.

Brigham's death at the end of "Afternoon" is quite as crucial as Joseph's death. Without Brigham, Zion seems less secure. "Evening" is the final movement of the novel, and Fisher's plan of organization emphasizes the passing of the generations. New generations look differently on celestial marriage and on the United Order, the communistic order with which the Saints had experimented. Fisher shows the crumbling of essential Mormon ideals by focusing not on a church leader but on the McBride family which represents three generations. The McBrides, Fisher's own characters, appear intermittently in all three sections. Maroni and Tim McBride, father and son, had followed Joseph through the worst persecutions in Missouri ("Morning"). Tim had been a Danite and had reported this group's horrible work to Joseph. Eventually Brigham had married the girl Tim loved. (She would have a higher station in heaven as Brigham's wife.) In "Afternoon" Brigham visited the starving boy Nephi McBride, Tim's son, in the early famine of the settlement; in "Evening" Nephi has great trouble with his wives, and finally one leaves him. Tim goes to jail for his faith in the doctrine. The McBrides hold fast to the gospel once delivered to the Saints, but they find no one with the courage of Brigham, and, when President Woodruff surrenders to federal demands, the McBrides feel the heart has gone out of their religion. The novel ends on a sad note as the McBrides, who were faithful from the beginning, leave the Salt Lake Zion—one more exodus.

The ending is not anti-climactic. Fisher wanted to tell more than the story of Joseph and Brigham; his story is of the children of God. By focusing on a humble family in the final section, the novel emphasizes the idea of latter-day saints—people with a vision and a need, who under Brigham's leadership were able to make a kingdom in the desert when they could find no refuge in their own country.

What makes these three large sections support the thesis of the novel is Fisher's talent for describing the action so central to an epic. The task is too big to expect many minute psychological portraits. Fisher can sketch Smith, Young, the McBrides in some detail, but the masses he can only suggest. Just as he is convincing with Smith and Young, can he be convincing in suggesting their followers. A large part of Fisher's success in having surrounded his characters with a sense of life is his skill in dialogue. They speak the language of the frontier, and Fisher knows that language well.

The skill in dialogue accounts also for much of the humor of the novel. Fisher's Saints are often humorous without knowing it—including Joseph. Although the reader is likely to be sympathizing with the Saints much of the time because of their troubles over celestial marriage, the institution provides Fisher with some pleasant humor. Brigham advises a man: "You'd better go read the apostle Paul. No man can be saved without a wife at his side—and the more the better" (499). Most of the Saints were not very familiar with the insides of their Bibles.

But never does Fisher present their ignorance arrogantly—it may be cause for laughter or pity but never for scorn. Fisher does not vilify them, for he is too aware of their persecutions. He reveals, however, Mormon errors, but with balance. For instance, the doctrine of blood atonement, as Brigham preached it, which indeed makes one wonder how much of the New Testament Brigham knew, is revealed but not exploited, nor given undue emphasis. Fisher is not a preacher in *Children of God*. In the final analysis, he presents his story to make his readers sympathetic to the Mormons (without making them believe Mormon dogma). He has indicated that the Mormon story has its epic dimensions.

VI   *The Course of Empire*

Common to the whole Americana, then, is the theme of the exploration of the West. In *Pemmican* Fisher portrays the company men of the North who preceded the real settlers and debauched the Indians. In *Tale of Valor* he celebrates the courage and wisdom of Lewis and Clark who helped establish the claim of the United States to the Oregon territory. *The Mothers* shows the migration to California—then Mexican territory—of American families who might have been a typical group had they had better leadership and better luck. The Mormons followed the Donners in the same year to the Salt Lake Basin, and in *Children of God* Fisher was the first novelist to do justice to their story. The ideals and leadership of the Mormon adventure are in contrast to their absence in another kind of Western settler, the miner, whom Fisher portrays in *City of Illusion.*

In all of these novels, except for *Pemmican,* Fisher focuses on actual persons and dramatizes known events. He introduces his minor characters so as not to distort the past—for his aim is to vitalize actual history. His novels are carefully researched; yet abundance of detail does not usually defeat the purpose of the narrative. The novels are not sentimental, but they reveal the vision and bravery in the settlement of the West as well as the abundant greed and barbarity.

Though the five books are not equally excellent, they are all engrossing. They are all action-packed, but they have a philosophic concern that raises them above the level of mere adventure stories. Moreover, the themes grow out of the action. These novels give Fisher an honored place among American historical novelists.

CHAPTER 7

Final Judgment

VARDIS FISHER—as this study has emphasized—has been an energetic writer. He has tried his hands at several kinds of novels, not to mention short stories, poetry, and an impressive body of non-fiction writing: a handbook for writers of fiction, a historical study of Meriwether Lewis' death, many essays, and a sizable amount of writing for the Federal Writers' Project. His output is more remarkable when one considers the hardship he found along much of the way. Yet the hardship was not completely unexpected, for by and large Fisher has devoted his life to writing for God, not Caesar. Since his days of graduate study at the University of Chicago, Fisher has had as his goal the creation of lasting books; and he has tirelessly run that hard course—even though he was a thousand times besieged by neglect and scorn and seldom given more than a pittance. He has been a Lewis and Clark, a Stendhal, and a Dock Hunter.

Though the toll on Fisher has sometimes been heavy, American literature has had something of decided value added to it. The gold has not been refined of all of its impurities; but, on several counts, our literary ledgers should place high value on Fisher's works. Of special significance for Americans, he has brought to the novel an authentic pioneer view and vigor. He is not only man on the frontier; he is the civilized writer schooled in great literature. His novels and stories of the Antelope country of Idaho not only make that region come alive, but—more forcefully than our pioneer stories can usually even intimate— portrays pioneer life in many phases, both its tragedy and its comedy, what day-by-day life means for adult and child. His first works, which indicated a genuine talent for characterizations, gave American letters vital characters in an area in which their lack in fiction had been so evident—convincing pioneers of the West.

As a writer whose first schooling, formal and otherwise, was in a lonely and primitive outpost of civilization, and as a trained scholar, Fisher was in an enviable position to render not only the Rocky Mountain frontier he knew but to research American historical novels as well. Fisher himself was aware of this, and it led him to his most serious flirtation with Caesar, for Fisher once conceived of American historical novels as a means to a purse and planned to alternate them with the *Testament of Man* novels (hoping to offer them to publishers as a package deal). But he could never really bring himself to the "pot boiler." *City of Illusion* and *Pemmican*, come closest to the charge; but even in them Fisher shows himself to be a serious writer. In fact, Fisher brings to the American historical novel exciting new possibilities for the form. The novels, after extensive research, were written in the spirit of achieving the greatest historical accuracy. As few novelists have done, Fisher has made historical accuracy his prime consideration, and he has proven that the stuff of history is adequate for a moving novel. The success of his "chronicle" novels owes much to his profound familiarity with the country and with the determined pioneers who settled Idaho and Utah. Although the historical novels do not have characters so roundly portrayed as do the Antelope novels, Fisher's Americana is an impressive panorama of the settling of the American West. On the basis of his presentation of that region alone—both in the sympathetic realism of a new regional literature for the Rocky Mountains and in researched historical novels—Vardis Fisher has earned himself a distinguished place in our literature.

A pioneer in producing lasting literature for the Far West, Fisher has also been pioneering in what must be regarded as one of the most ambitious of modern literary undertakings—a desire to show the past in the present by tracing the development of man's religious conscience throughout the ages. Fisher has again surpassed the average historical novel. He not only charges the historical novelist with researching events of wars, economics, politics, persons, but a deep reading into anthropology, psychology, and the higher criticism. Fisher has himself felt the immensity of his ideals and has thought that he began the series too late in life (he was scarcely forty when he started the project). The resulting novels certainly command attention, though they are not perfect as novels and most of them are not likely to capture the popular imagination. Readers may be annoyed at the excessive exposition, abrupt transitions, and erratic punctuation; and it is certain that Fisher retold Vridar's story more than he should have in the series, for his didactic slant gives the *Testament* a marked imbalance. The novels increasingly lead the reader to the conviction that Fisher has not revealed the whole of the Western religious heritage: the ring of history—a convincing picture of an area and satisfactory devices for presenting factual background—is not present in the later volumes in the same force as in the American historicals, though as partial defense of Fisher one must say that the *Testament* becomes increasingly symbolic. This is not to question that the novels are carefully researched but to assert that all of the Vridars and their creator never grasp the dynamism of Christianity, which is also a part of history. Fisher has never seen that, though Christianity has been a religion of the desert, it has also been a religion of the valleys of vision. Nowhere does he give a convincing portrait of a George Herbert, who lived in the beauty of holiness, nor of a Jonathan Edwards in all of his complexity and stature. These people are beyond Fisher—who might have recalled Cabell and the dynamic illusion. There is a poetic mysticism and beauty Fisher failed to see.

Nevertheless, one should grant that much of the *Testament* is imagined as experience. Even in a discursive novel like *A Goat for Azazel* one feels Fisher knows people. And because Fisher frequently presents basic human hungers so convincingly, the art of the *Testament* sometimes runs very high. It is no small tribute to Fisher that the most elemental characters come to life. Indeed, *Darkness and the Deep* and *The Golden Rooms* are the best novels of their kind. Fisher's excellence in showing action and violence as well as compassion marks the *Testament*, as well as the Antelope novels and the Americana. And nowhere will the historical novelist find the challenge to penetrating study greater than in the *Testament* nor will its readers find a greater spur to thought.

This challenge is part and parcel of Fisher's work as an autobiographical novelist. As a conclusion to the *Testament*, the gigantic *Orphans in Gethsemane* presents the vision and theme of the entire *Testament* in its re-creation of the life of its creator. And *Orphans* is an autobiographical novel decidedly worthy of the attention of the serious reader. It is in part a re-telling of the Vridar Hunter tetralogy which critics of the 1930's had to praise even when they were infuriated. But the first volume of the tetralogy, *In Tragic Life,* escaped the strong protests, and immediately became a classic. Perhaps the praise the tetralogy got in the 1930's was due in part to its observably increasing concern with social problems, but this was certainly not the cause of the praise for the first volume. The interest in the tetralogy in itself suggests that *Orphans* has not nearly had its due, for it significantly improves on the tetralogy. The placing of Vridar against our most crucial myths has raised his stature significantly and heightened the universality of the novel, for Vridar does suggest age-old strivings. In addition, his story is a moving panorama of the thoughtful writer in the twentieth century. In a new way, Vridar's story is a challenge to greater humanity, to greater wisdom, and to a more joyous life.

In a prolific career, Fisher has not been a static writer, and he cannot, therefore, be easily labeled. His work has more complexity than summary treatments of him have usually indicated. If he is a hard-boiled Naturalist, he is also a humanitarian—and though many critics missed it—a humorist. If he sometimes is overly didactic (he can be a superb essayist and has written challengingly on the craft of the novel in *God or Caesar?*), he has written novels in which he has been quite detached—even in novels before *Children of God*—unlike what his reviewers have declared. He has not only written novels on many subjects, but he has experimented with form; he has unfortunately, however, never developed the technical excellence of most of our major figures. Though he has not always written with grace, he is sometimes a poet and his style is usually clean. He has written a few finely chiseled short stories—especially those set in Antelope, and if he has not done more with the genre, it is not from lack of ability. As poet, essayist, and novelist, Fisher is a writer of range, imagination, and mind.

In view of his accomplishments and his failures, it seems likely that Fisher will continue to be read—for what he has tried to do as well as for what he has done. One does not see a revival of interest in Fisher of the scope of a Fitzgerald revival. Clearly Fisher is not every man's writer, and it is quite conceivable that readers will approve him in one kind of novel—or genre—and not in another, in itself a tribute to his range. And of course, Fisher is a masculine writer, one for the tough-minded. His works are not for the squeamish, nor on the other hand would some do at all for readers with no interest in more intellectual matters. Fisher has never tried to titillate the glands, but he does suggest that in all of life the mind could be better used. Though modern prejudice is against the intruding author and the didactic and though Fisher's Naturalism is sometimes harsh—even overdone—the power of his vision and his ability to portray human character should mean a continuous and growing number of readers.

Notes and References

Preface

1. Unpublished letter of Elizabeth Nowell to Vardis Fisher, June 20, 1935.

2. Unpublished letter of Elizabeth Nowell to Vardis Fisher, August 13, 1950.

3. Comparing Wolfe and Fisher is now critical commonplace—fostered in reviews of Fisher and carried into critical articles by John Peale Bishop and George Snell. Recently Wolfe and Fisher are compared by John O. Lyons, *The College Novel in America* (Carbondale, Illinois, 1962), p. 87.

Chapter One

1. The information in this chapter has been gathered from Stanley J. Kunitz and Howard Haycroft, *Twentieth Century Authors* (New York, 1942) and Kunitz's *First Supplement* (1955); "Idaho Individualist," *MD: Medical Newsmagazine*, V (November, 1961), 143-46, which is reprinted in *Arts and Sciences* (Spring, 1962), pp. 9-12; and Fisher's several articles published throughout his career, mainly: "Hometown Revisited 13: The Antelope Hills, Idaho," *Tomorrow*, IX (December, 1949), 18-23; "A Trivial Excursion in Modesty," *The Antioch Review*, II (1942), 122-28; "Novel Writing Is My Trade," *Tomorrow*, IX (August, 1950), 5-10; and from an interview with Fisher at the Hagerman ranch and from Fisher's correspondence with me and from my study of the Fisher correspondence at the Yale University Library.

2. Fisher writes that though he holds his paternal grandmother responsible for his name, his sister and her daughter have traced the family line (for reasons of Mormon doctrine) and discovered that the name Vardis goes back to the eighteenth century and that Alvero (the middle name he hated and dropped) has also appeared before. Letter to the author, February 11, 1963.

3. "My Experience with Thomas Wolfe," *Tomorrow*, X (April, 1951), 25. Readers interested in Fisher's views on Wolfe will also wish to read "Thomas Wolfe and Maxwell Perkins," *Tomorrow*, X (July, 1951), 21-25. Fisher deals with Wolfe throughout *God or Caesar?*

4. Russell Krauss, "Replacing Tom Wolfe," *Thomas Wolfe at Washington Square*, eds. Thomas Clark Pollock and Oscar Cargill (New York, 1954), p. 147. Note, however, that Krauss pushes the date of *In Tragic Life* too close to *Look Homeward, Angel*. Wolfe may, of course, have voiced this opinion of Fisher, but not while the two were teaching at Washington Square College. Fisher refutes Krauss's story.

5. Elizabeth Nowell, ed. *The Letters of Thomas Wolfe* (New York, 1956), p. 768.

6. *MD* reports a story of a unique party game which Fisher introduced to colleagues at Montana. Players drank until inhibitions were relaxed, then began spinning the bottle. He at whom the bottle pointed had to answer with absolute truth any question he might be asked. Fisher says the story is grossly exaggerated. An account of the game is also in Fisher's novel *Forgive Us Our Virtues*. He still holds to the therapeutic value of liquor, discussed in *No Villian Need Be*.

7. Vardis Fisher, *The Caxton Printers in Idaho: A Short History* (Cincinnati, 1945), p. 21.

8. E. Current-Garcia, "American Panorama," *Prairie Schooner*, XII (Summer, 1938), 90.

9. E. Current-Garcia, "Writers in the 'Sticks,'" *Prairie Schooner*, XII (Winter, 1938), 302.

Chapter Two

1. Lionel Trilling, "Freud and Literature," *The Liberal Imagination* (New York, 1950), p. 37.

2. Vardis Fisher, "A Trivial Excursion in Modesty," *The Antioch Review*, II (1942), 126.

3. *Ibid.*, pp. 125-26.

4. Vardis Fisher, "The Novelist and His Background," *Western Folklore*, XII (1953), 3.

5. Alan Swallow, "The Mavericks," *Critique: Studies in Modern Fiction*, II (Winter, 1959), 83.

6. To minimize the number of footnotes in this book, I include page numbers of Fisher's novels within the body. Editions referred to are the ones cited in the bibliography. Titles are abbreviated except for short stories, which are cited in *Love and Death*.

7. Vardis Fisher, *God or Caesar?* (Caldwell, Idaho, 1953), p. 84.

8. Post card to the author, May 9, 1962.

9. Vivian E. Fisher, *Auto-correctivism: The Psychology of Nervousness* (Caldwell, Idaho, 1937), pp. 39-40; 57-70.

10. Letter to the author, April 19, 1962.

11. Vardis Fisher, *God or Caesar?*, pp. 147-49.
12. Oscar Cargill, *Intellectual America* (New York, 1941), p. 736.
13. Vardis Fisher, "The Novelist and his Background," p. 3.

Chapter Three

1. Vardis Fisher, "The Novelist and his Background," pp. 3-4.
2. Fred T. Marsh, "Vardis Fisher, Modern Rousseau," New York *Times Book Review*, March 8, 1936, p. 2.
3. "Alan Swallow Interviewing Vardis Fisher on the Testament of Man," *Inland* (Autumn, 1959), p. 28.
4. Vardis Fisher, *God or Caesar?*, p. 20.
5. *Ibid.*, p. 21.
6. *Ibid.*
7. *Ibid.*, p. 24.
8. Quoted in Vardis Fisher, *God or Caesar?*, p. 82.
9. Vardis Fisher, *God or Caesar?*, p. 203.
10. *Ibid.*, p. 56.
11. Quoted in Vardis Fisher, *God or Caesar?*, p. 83.
12. E. M. Forster, *Aspects of the Novel* (New York, 1927), pp. 65-82.
13. I consider stylistic changes in some detail in my Ph.D. dissertation *Vardis Fisher's Story of Vridar Hunter: A Study in Theory and Revision* (Michigan, 1962), pp. 161-97.

Chapter Four

1. Vardis Fisher, *God or Caesar?*, p. 89.
2. Alan Swallow, "The Mavericks," p. 83 .
3. Thomas C. Chubb, "History Without Shading," New York *Times Book Review*, December 7, 1958, p. 48.

Chapter Five

1. Vardis Fisher, "Hometown Revisited 13: The Antelope Hills, Idaho," *Tomorrow*, IX (December, 1949), 18.
2. Harold G. Merriam, ed., *Northwest Verse, An Anthology* (Caldwell, Idaho, 1931), pp. 137-39; Bess Foster Smith, ed., *Sunlit Peaks, An Anthology of Idaho Verse* (Caldwell, Idaho, 1931), pp. 74-75.
3. Vardis Fisher, "Hometown Revisited," p. 18.
4. John Peale Bishop, "The Strange Case of Vardis Fisher," *The Collected Essays of John Peale Bishop* (New York, 1948), pp. 56-65.

5. George Snell, *Shapers of American Fiction* (New York, 1947), pp. 276-78.

6. Joseph Warren Beach, *The American Novel 1920-1940* (New York, 1960), p. 244.

Chapter Six

1. *The Idaho Encyclopedia* Federal Writers' Project, Director: Vardis Fisher (Caldwell, Idaho, 1938), p. 82.

2. Swallow, p. 84.

3. "West of the Mississippi: An Interview with Frederick Manfred," *Critique: Studies in Modern Fiction*, II (Winter, 1959), 44.

4. Swallow, p. 80.

5. *Encyclopedia Britannica*, 1959 edition, Vol. XI, p. 861. Interestingly, *Encyclopedia Americana*, 1959 edition, Vol. XIV, praises the Hudson's Bay Company's treatment of the Indian in its early history but is silent on this latter aspect of the record.

6. Ernest E. Leisey, *The American Historical Novel* (Norman, 1950), p. 145.

7. Carl Van Doren, *The American Novel 1789-1939* (New York, 1945), p. 349.

8. Fisher, of course, was very aware of the continuing power of the Mormon church. His point was simply that after the Woodruff proclamation, the kind of power changed.

9. Vardis Fisher, *God or Caesar?*, pp. 241-42.

10. David B. Davis, " 'Children of God': An Historian's Evaluation," *Western Humanities Review*, VIII (Winter, 1953-54), 49-56.

11. Bernard DeVoto, "The Centennial of Mormonism: A Study in Utopia and Dictatorship," *Forays and Rebuttals* (Boston, 1936), pp. 77-137. Readers wishing to study the matter more carefully will also be interested in DeVoto's treatment of the Mormons in *Year of Decision, 1846* and in *Mark Twain's America*.

12. Bernard DeVoto, "Millennial Million," *The Saturday Review of Literature*, XX (August 26, 1939), 14.

13. Vardis Fisher, "Children of God," *Oregon Historical Quarterly*, XLI (June, 1940), 126-28.

14. Alfred Kazin, "Our Last Authentic Frontier Novelist," New York *Herald Tribune Book Review*, August 27, 1939, p. 3.

Selected Bibliography

PRIMARY SOURCES

A. *The Vridar Hunter Tetralogy*

Publ:shed jointly by Caxton Printers, Caldwell, Idaho, and Doubleday, Doran & Company, Garden City, New York. Caxton has the first editions.

In Tragic Life (1932).
Passions Spin the Plot (1934).
We Are Betrayed (1935).
No Villian Need Be (1936).

B. *The Testament of Man*

Darkness and the Deep. New York: The Vanguard Press, 1943.
The Golden Rooms. New York: The Vanguard Press, 1944.
Intimations of Eve. New York: The Vanguard Press, 1946.
Adam and the Serpent. New York: The Vanguard Press, 1947.
The Divine Passion. New York: The Vanguard Press, 1948.
The Valley of Vision. New York: Abelard Press, 1951.
The Island of the Innocent. New York: Abelard Press, 1952.
Jesus Came Again. Denver: Alan Swallow, 1956.
A Goat for Azazel. Denver: Alan Swallow, 1956.
Peace Like a River. Denver: Alan Swallow, 1957.
My Holy Satan. Denver: Alan Swallow, 1958.
Orphans in Gethsemane. Denver: Alan Swallow, 1960.

C. *Other Novels*

Toilers of the Hills. Boston and New York: Houghton Mifflin Co., 1928.
Dark Bridwell. Boston and New York: Houghton Mifflin Co., 1931.
April: A Fable of Love. Caldwell, Idaho: The Caxton Printers, 1937.
Forgive Us Our Virtues: A Comedy of Evasions. Caldwell, Idaho: The Caxton Printers, 1938.
Children of God: An American Epic. New York: Harper and Brothers, 1939.
The Mothers: An American Saga of Courage. New York: The Vanguard Press, 1943.

City of Illusion. New York: Harper and Brothers, 1941.
Pemmican. Garden City, New York: Doubleday & Co., Inc., 1956.
Tale of Valor. Garden City, New York: Doubleday & Co., Inc., 1958.

D. *Short Stories*

Love and Death. Garden City, New York: Doubleday & Co., Inc., 1959.

E. *Non-Fiction*

George Meredith's Literary Reputation: 1850-1885. Unpublished Ph.D. Dissertation, University of Chicago, 1925.
Sonnets to an Imaginary Madonna. New York: Harold Vinal, 1927.
The Caxton Printers in Idaho: A Short History. Cincinnati: Society of Bibliosophers, 1945.
The Neurotic Nightingale. Milwaukee: Casanova Press, 1935.
God or Caesar? The Writing of Fiction for Beginners. Caldwell, Idaho: The Caxton Printers, 1953.
Thomas Wolfe as I Knew Him and Other Essays. Denver: Alan Swallow, 1963.

F. *Books for Federal Writers' Project edited by and largely work of Fisher, all published by The Caxton Printers*

Idaho, A Guide in Word and Picture (1937).
The Idaho Encyclopedia (1938).
Idaho Lore (1939).

SECONDARY SOURCES

BENÉT, WILLIAM ROSE. "A Realistic Novel of Adolescent Struggles," *The Saturday Review of Literature*, X (January 6, 1934), 394. A review of protest and irritation.
BISHOP, JOHN PEALE. "The Strange Case of Vardis Fisher," *The Collected Essays of John Peale Bishop*. New York: Charles Scribner's Sons, 1948, pp. 56-65. Written in the 1930's (*The Southern Review:* Autumn, 1937, pp. 348-59), this essay compares Fisher with Caldwell, Faulkner, and Wolfe.
CURRENT-GARCIA, E. "Writers in the 'Sticks,'" *Prairie Schooner*, XII (Winter, 1938), 294-309. An unimpassioned consideration of Fisher's work along with that of other writers involved in the Federal Writers' Project.
DEVOTO, BERNARD. "Millennial Million," *The Saturday Review of*

Literature, XX (August 26, 1939), 41. Vigorous praise for *Children of God* as Fisher's masterpiece.

FOOTE, ELLIS. "The Unholy Testator," *American Book Collector*, XIV (September, 1963), 9-12. A colorful portrait; though exaggerated, it catches several facets of Fisher's personality.

HOLMES, OPAL LAUREL, "Once In A Wifetime," *American Book Collector*, XIV (September 1963), 13-14. Mrs. Vardis Fisher gives a wife's view of her husband as man and as artist.

"Idaho Individualist," *MD, Medical Newsmagazine*, V (November, 1961), 143-46. This helpful summary of Fisher's career is reprinted in *Arts and Sciences* (Spring, 1962), pp. 9-12.

KAZIN, ALFRED, "Our Last Authentic Frontier Novelist," New York *Herald Tribune Book Review*, August 27, 1939, p. 3. One of the more cautious reviews of *Children of God*, it should be set next to DeVoto's. The review is valuable also in light of artistic weaknesses of the *Testament*.

KELLOG, GEORGE. "Vardis Fisher: A Bibliography," *The Bookmark*, supplement to Vol. XIII, No. 3. The Library, University of Idaho, Moscow: March, 1961. Valuable to the scholar in identifying little known articles about Fisher (most of negligible value) as well as obscure articles by him.

MANFRED, FREDERICK. "Hareb's Temptation," New York *Times Book Review*, December 8, 1957, p. 40. Strong praise for the *Testament of Man* by a contemporary novelist.

MARGARICK, P. "Vardis Fisher and His Testament of Man," *American Book Collector*, XIV (September, 1963), 20-24. Outlines the *Testament*.

MARSH, FRED T. "In Tragic Life," New York *Times Book Review*, December 25, 1932, p. 4. A judicious review that prepared the way for Fisher's fame in the 1930's.

————. "A Long Quest for the Good Life," New York *Times Book Review*, January 20, 1935, p. 4. Reviews the accomplishment of the tetralogy.

REIN, DAVID. *Vardis ·Fisher: Challenge to Evasion*. Chicago: Black Cat Press, Normandie House, 1937. Interesting example of Marxist criticism of the 1930's.

SNELL, GEORGE. *Shapers of American Fiction*. New York: E. P. Dutton & Co., Inc., 1943, pp. 276-88. The only critical survey of American fiction which ranks Fisher among our major authors.

STEGNER, WALLACE, "Forgive Us Our Neuroses," *Rocky Mountain Review*, II (Spring, 1938), 1-3. A former student warns Fisher that the didactic harms his work.

SWALLOW, ALAN. "The Mavericks," *Critique: Studies in Modern Fiction,* II (Winter, 1959), 79-84. Reprinted in Swallow's *An Editor's Essays of Two Decades,* Experiment Press, 1962. Swallow re-opens the case for Vardis Fisher.

VAN DOREN, MARK. "Got Wot," *The Nation,* CXLII (March 11, 1936), 324-25. Takes Fisher to task for the weak ending of the tetralogy. A valuable statement.

————. "A Twelve-Cylinder Idyl," *The Nation,* CXLIV (February 20, 1937), 214. Reviews *April* favorably. Interesting for analysis of Fisher's accomplishment to date.

Index

Index

Index